# Money and Good Intentions Are Not Enough

# Money and Good Intentions Are Not Enough

*or, Why a Liberal Democrat Thinks States Need Both Competition and Community*

John E. Brandl

Brookings Institution Press
*Washington, D. C.*

Copyright © 1998 by

THE BROOKINGS INSTITUTION
*1775 Massachusetts Ave., N.W. Washington, D.C. 20036*

*Library of Congress Cataloging in-Publication data*
Brandl, John E.
    Money and good intentions are not enough, or, Why a liberal democrat thinks states need both competition and community / John E. Brandl
        p.  cm.
    Includes bibliographical references and index.

    ISBN 0-8157-1060-7 (cloth : alk. paper)
    ISBN 0-8157-1059-3 (pbk. : alk. paper)
    1. State governments—United States. I. Title. II. Title: Money and good intentions are not enough  III. Title: Why a liberal democrat thinks states need both competition and community
    JK2443 .B77   1998
    321.02'3'0973—ddc21                                97-45313
                                                            CIP


9 8 7 6 5 4 3 2 1

The paper used in this publication meets the minimum requirements of the American National Standard for Information Sciences—Permanence of Paper for Printed Library Materials: ANSI Z39.48-1984.

Typeset in Palatino

Composition by Cynthia Stock
Silver Spring, Maryland

Printed by R. R. Donnelley & Sons Co.
Harrisonburg, Virginia

*For Chris, Kate, and Amy*

# Contents

1   An Agenda for the States     1
    A Policy Requires a Theory   3
    The Book's Mode of Argument   8
    An Outline of the Book   11

2   What State Governments Do Now and Will Do in the Future     16
    What State Governments Do Now   16
    Fiscal Prospects for the States   19
    Conclusion   27

3   Do State Taxpayers Get Their Money's Worth?     29
    The Dismal Record of Elementary and Secondary Education   30
    Spending on Schools Can Make a Difference   32
    The Inefficacy of Other State-Funded Bureaus   35
    The Record of State Government Enterprises   38
    State Grants to Local Governments   41
    Conclusion   44

4   Why State Governments Are Unacceptably Ineffective     46
    How the Founders Sought to Harness Self-Interest   47
    How Faulty Theories Have Contributed to Governmental Inefficiency   49
    A New Understanding of Government Failure in the States   55
    How Legislatures Operate   57
    How Governments and Private Markets Fail in Like Fashion   63
    Conclusion   73

5   Toward State Government That Works: Aligning Private
    and Public Purposes                                          76
      Policymaking as the Design of Government   76
      A Menu for Public Policy Design   80
      The Importance of the New Economics of Organization   87
      Who Oversees the Overseers?   88
      Conclusion   91

6   Beyond Incentives: Community as Policy                       92
      The Communitarian Critique      94
      Varieties of Community      96
      Conclusion      114

7   Competition and Community: Policies for the States          115
      Using Competition   116
      The Three Kinds of Competition-Inducing Policies   122
      Using Community   123
      The Complementarity of Competition and Community   127
      Choice and Community: An Agenda for the States   129
      Conclusion   132

8   Reprise                                                      134

Notes      143

Index      173

Tables

2-1.   Final Goods and Services and Income Transfers Funded by State
       Governments, 1990                                         18
2-2.   Annual Growth in U.S. Output per Worker, 1950–2005        21
3-1.   Reported Differences between Public and Private Costs for
       Production of Services                                    37
4-1.   How Private and Public Production of Goods and Services Fails   64
7-1.   Three Policies for Introducing Competition into the Production
       of Services Provided by Government                        122
7-2.   Designs for Policymaking: Competition as a Response
       to Market and Government Failure                          124
7-3.   Using Competition and Community to Accomplish the Main
       Responsibilities of State Government                      130

# Preface

This book has been brewing for most of my life, though I didn't apprehend its message until a few years ago. Its central argument—that only competition and community can dependably channel the efforts of free people to public purposes—emerged from several sources. These include life in a happy family; education by Benedictines; the professional study of economics; involvement as a federal government official in policy evaluations that, though well conducted, had little effect; attempts as a legislator to craft programs of lasting efficacy; and numerous visits to Central Europe, where a grandiose pipedream had cast aside both competition and community and brought ruin upon whole countries.

After my family I owe most to the Benedictines. Numerous sisters and monks have demonstrated to me the wonders of community. Some, in particular the redoubtable Sister Annerose Wokurka and Father Martin Schirber, also taught me to see the need for and power of markets in a world in which not everyone is as generous and other-minded as they.

Since this is a work not of analysis but of synthesis, the ideas of many are stitched together here. I received wise counsel from MaryEllen Berman, Harry C. Boyte, Donald Brandl, Gene Brandl, Tom Dewar, Michael Finn, Thomas Fiutak, John Freeman, Daniel Gifford, Steven Gold, Gerald Heaney, Ted Kolderie, Robert Kudrle, Paul C. Light, Joe Nathan, David Osborne, Paul E. Peterson,

G. Edward Schuh, Frank J. Thompson, Vin Weber, John M. Yinger, and anonymous reviewers.

Several research assistants, especially Debora Bednarz, Ronald St. Pierre, David Marcotte, and Susan Scott, helped find ideas. Students at the Humphrey Institute and at the Warsaw School of Economics were inspiring.

Lori Sturdevant, when she was a reporter for the Minneapolis *Tribune*, was the first to ask me to say what my agenda for the state of Minnesota is. The late Robert Spaeth first suggested I write this book. Bob was not only the most broadly learned person I've known; he also was always eager to discuss the ideas in the book.

While writing the book I imagined two friends, John Adams and Charles Neerland, one a professor and the other an active citizen, looking over my shoulder. Nearly every page here contains improvements wrought by Nancy Davidson of Brookings, a splendid editor. I also thank Gail Thorin for editing the manuscript, Carlotta Ribar for proofreading the pages, and Jane Maddocks for preparing the index.

My wife Rochelle lovingly coaxed and prodded.

# Money and Good Intentions
# Are Not Enough

# 1

# *An Agenda for the States*

AMERICA needs better from its state governments if the country is to thrive in the future. The states are not meeting their grand responsibilities, and for what they do accomplish, the citizenry is not getting its money's worth. The remedies usually offered—cut or add to the budget, or exhort civil servants to be more entrepreneurial, or seek tougher managers or worthier politicians or smarter bureaucrats—would not provide substantial, lasting improvement. In this book I develop an explanation, drawn from contemporary social science, for how government operates and why it blunders. From that critique emerges an agenda of policies aimed at making government more productive and more gratifying, not only to its workers but especially to its citizens. Some of the argument of the book is as relevant to other levels of government as it is to the states. I apply the reasoning to state government because it has been relatively neglected by scholars in recent times and because after twelve years as a legislator in Minnesota I have more experience there than in Washington.

Government fails when its officials, or persons in a position to influence them, frustrate public purposes by gaining benefits for themselves at the expense of others. Indeed, the first measure of a government should be its degree of success at preventing people from seizing unjustified advantages. I maintain that for most of what government does—the production of services—its policymaking responsibility is to arrange affairs in such a way that both private citizens and public employees can accomplish public purposes as well while acting ordinarily and freely in ways that accomplish their own objectives.[1]

Two efficacious and self-disciplining means of accomplishing this conjunction of purposes are available: harnessing self-interest through competition—*choice*, and transcending self-interest by encouraging affiliations that inspire altruistic behavior—*community*. Successful production of services depends on one or both of these meta-policies. While industrious workers, skilled management, and dynamic leadership are desirable, they are not always reliably accessible. Competition and community do not substitute for government. They are the instruments through which government facilitates the working out of public purposes by a free people.

State government is frequently unproductive. Increases in spending often yield insignificant results. Funds intended for one purpose are used for others. Usually this is not so much the perverse achievement of villains as misallocation by a system gone awry. As we will see, the rules and bureaucratic incentives that pervade government often permit and even encourage ordinary people to act in ways that protect themselves while harming others.

Occasionally one hears the claim that productivity, getting our money's worth, should be expected of private firms, but government is about something else: government's responsibilities are sublime and thus should be beyond the dismal purview of economizers; or since government must accommodate competing notions about what its objectives should be, frugality in meeting those objectives is irrelevant or trivial, the least of its worries. Nonsense! State government is so important and so costly that it must be made more productive. Not to do so would jeopardize our future as weighty tasks continue to be performed poorly.

Elementary and secondary education best illustrates this point and will be cited throughout the book as the main example. It is by far the largest expenditure item of the states; much research has been conducted on its efficacy; and, as we will see, its problems are representative. From my high school years in the 1950s to the present, America's spending per elementary and secondary student has increased twentyfold.[2] That figure is misleading, of course, because of the inflation that occurred in those years. Still, in real terms, that is, after factoring out inflation, spending per student nearly quintupled. During the lifetime of my children and the other college students of the 1990s, America's real spending per elementary and secondary pupil has doubled.[3] Think of it; the schools devote twice as much of society's resources to a student now as was the case a mere quarter of a century ago. Would anyone argue that today's young people leave high school twice as well educated in any sense? Schooling is a typical governmental activity. State government is not giving citizens value for money.

If what states do were unnecessary or inconsequential, the appropriate response to this situation would be obvious: cut government; cut any part of it; cut it across the board. However, schooling is representative not only because it is unsatisfactorily carried out but also because it matters. The education of young people is the main opportunity states have to influence the future. At present nothing should worry policymakers more than the development of our youngsters. Their level of learning does not compare well with the achievement of students in many other countries, nor is it commensurate with the needs of the future. Most other state-funded services are like schooling: they are meant to confront important and pressing issues, but they do so disappointingly or at an unacceptably high cost. From job training to road construction to janitorial services to traffic signal maintenance, some state and local governments pay four, five, even eight times as much as others. In the face of exorbitant costs and in the absence of demonstrated productivity improvements, the discontent of citizens with government is apt to persist, and societal objectives of decisive importance will not be attained.

Thus the need for an agenda that is an explanation of the current predicament and a derivative and coherent set of proposed remedial policies.

## A Policy Requires a Theory

To propose a policy is to argue that a government action will bring about a desired outcome. This is equivalent to saying that a government policy embodies a hypothesis that an action X will yield an outcome Y.

For example, some economists believe that welfare recipients would freely work additional hours for pay if they were allowed to keep more of their earnings rather than, as has often been the case, having most of their pay subtracted from their welfare grants. Other people maintain that recipients are motivated to get off welfare even if their financial circumstances are not improved in the process. These different views—hypotheses emerging from different theories of human behavior—lead to different policies. If the latter view better captures how welfare recipients act, then a policy of cutting benefits as recipients earn money on a job would leave them no less inclined to work for pay. If, though, the former hypothesis is true, then sharply reducing welfare payments as recipients earn money is likely to dissuade them from working if they can receive money without doing so. Theories underlie policies; different theories have different implications for policy.

Now, there are those who find it hard to swallow the notion that policymaking requires theory. Some down-home politicians insist that pragmatism is more important than theoretical knowledge. In their opinion, theory is abstract, irrelevant; making policy, they say, requires horse sense. The practical person disparages academic abstraction as unrealistic, even as many a professor dismisses common sense as unsophisticated. But it is foolish to think of a person or a society as benefiting by only one or the other of these modes of thinking. Each involves using theory.

For a dozen years I served simultaneously as a member of the Minnesota legislature and a professor at one of the nation's leading research universities. Part of the satisfaction of legislative life lies in associating with people possessed of a great variety of appealing qualities that, though they may be found at a university, are not officially valued and rewarded there: courage, loyalty, passion, coolness in adversity, good humor, occasionally modesty, and, yes, common sense. But whether genius or nitwit, a politician cannot get by without theory.

To propose a policy is, whether one acknowledges it or not, to hold a theory that indicates why the policy can be expected to be efficacious. In this context a theory is a conjecture or explanation of how the object of inquiry operates and how it can be influenced by a government action. If the theory is inductively achieved through experience we call it common sense.

Often the theory underlying a policy is implicit and ad hoc, but, whatever one's basis for predicting a policy's effects, it must survive testing. A person who, on the way to work some morning, concocts an explanation for the deficiencies in energy policy or for that which ails the highway department, by noon will likely find the conjecture unpersuasive. Academic influence on public affairs lies in devising and testing theories of lasting explanatory power.

John Maynard Keynes, the author of what in Western countries became the most influential macroeconomic theory of this century, realized that the ideas of professors have effect to the extent that they become the means by which citizens and their politicians think about issues. Ironically, the legislator who flouts newfangled theory may be doing so out of attachment to an outdated conception of yesteryear's academician. Said Keynes: "The ideas of economists and political philosophers both when they are right and when they are wrong, are more powerful than is commonly understood. Indeed, the world is ruled by little else. Practical men, who believe themselves to be quite exempt from any intellectual influences, are usually the slaves of some defunct economist."[4] If Keynes were alive today and if he had a trace of modesty, a trait not detected in him by his contemporaries, he might concede that in the 1990s his own theory of a half century ago illustrates that point. New economic theories are superseding that of Keynes.

Much state policy rests on discredited theories, some of which are derived from common sense and others from academic research. The absence of supporting evidence for these theories highlights the need for new ideas.

The most widely, if implicitly, invoked hypothesis underlying state policy is this: if more dollars are appropriated to education (or welfare or highways or whatever), corresponding and appropriate outcomes will occur more frequently. That theory lies behind politicians' pledges of more funds to this or that project as a sign of determination to generate better results. The sad example of American education exposes the vacuousness of the notion that spending can be counted on to yield desired outcomes. Fundamental to improving state government is the replacement of that entrenched idea with policies containing a strong connection between spending and expected results.

In the academy's prevailing style of theory construction, hypotheses are derived by means of an explicit logic from a set of assumptions.[5] For example, some contemporary social scientists assume that government bureaucrats attempt to maximize the size of their bureaus or otherwise enhance their own positions. Reasoning from that assumption, social scientists then predict how bureaus populated by such persons would act in various situations. One such prediction, at odds with the theory that spending automatically yields results, is, unsurprisingly, that some of the funds granted to a bureau are likely to be devoted to the interests of the bureaucrats rather than to the funders' purposes for the bureau. (A bureau is an organization that gets its funding not from customers but from a sponsor, typically a legislature. Its members are not permitted to keep for themselves any difference between revenues and expenditures, and a bureau can receive its funds whether or not the ultimate recipients of its services are satisfied with them.) Thus bureaus are expected often to spend more than is necessary to carry out some projects and to produce a different mix of products than if they were only responding to the wishes of politicians and citizens. An example of this occurred recently in my south Minneapolis neighborhood, where a half-million dollars were spent on refurbishing the athletic field of the local high school, while some of the science laboratories there exist in a time warp going back a quarter-century. During those decades none of the sports played on the now-modernized field had undergone as much change as any of the sciences taught in the laboratories. Underlining the message sent by the school system that it has its own purposes apart from educating the students and welcoming the participation of the local citizens, a locked gate prevents residents of the neighborhood from jogging on the track around the field.

Economics is the most elegantly developed and easily applied of the social sciences that predict human behavior based on an assumption of self-interest. Individuals are assumed to act consistently: consumers strive to maximize the enjoyment they get from their spending, producers maximize their profit, bureaucrats their budget, politicians their odds of reelection. From that assumption are drawn hypotheses about what individuals, firms, bureaus, and legislatures would do in a variety of circumstances, such as the levying of a tax, the appearance of a competitor in a market, or the imposition of a rule on a bureau or politician.

In those situations and others, private individuals and government officials act. State governments tax liquor, accept bids for construction of a highway, tell a principal what courses to offer in her school, prohibit certain gifts to legislators. The policy is undertaken with an expectation that people's behavior will change as predicted by the theory underlying the policy. That is the meaning of a policy.

Self-concerned consumers are predicted, of course, to buy less of the product when a liquor tax is imposed. Contractors having to compete for business are predicted to be less likely to gouge customers. The theory predicts that a principal will not necessarily do what she is told if it does not conform with her desires. Similar reactions are expected from politicians, especially if they can conceal some aspects of their behavior. In each of these circumstances other theories predict other responses. Empirical measurement of results can show one theory to be a better predictor of actual behavior, thus indicating one policy to be more powerful than others.

Advocates of the meaning of *theory* used here disagree as to whether its assumptions must be realistic or whether, rather, the sole test of a theory is how well it predicts.[6] (Are humans the narrowly self-concerned drones of the economists' assumption, or is that question irrelevant as long as economic theory accurately predicts the outcome of a tax or deregulation or proclamation of a rule?) I take predictability of results to be an important gauge of the adequacy of a theory. However, I will examine some of the shortcomings of theories that are based on the assumption of self-interest.[7] For example, this society suffers to the extent that people come to pattern their actions on the self-interest theory, justifying greed by claiming that the country's prosperity is due to economic and political systems that presume self-interested behavior.[8] I will show that an alert government can meet its responsibilities by fostering the beneficence generated in such institutions as families, neighborhoods, and religious organizations.

Another objection to the use of economic thinking in policymaking comes from those of my students who are concerned lest they, by acquiring the skills of the economist and statistician, become uncaring and conservative, devoid of compassion and a healthy skepticism of the powers that be. One can be either quantitative or humane, they worry, and they know which they would rather be. But an empirically verified hypothesis need not be used in antidemocratic fashion. It can be of service to the poor and the excluded, which I hope will be the case for the agenda developed here.

Far from ratifying ineffective current institutions, the critique contained herein argues that institutional redesign is essential if states are to meet their responsibilities and that policymaking is critical in the design and use of effective institutions. Some readers might think it obvious to understand policymaking in this way. I remind them that the vogue today is rather to perceive policymaking as priority setting and budget allocation, neither of which is necessarily related to acceptable results.

There is no getting around it: to offer an agenda is to hold a theory. A policy reflects a theory that a governmental action will yield a desired result.

## The Book's Mode of Argument

Throughout much of American history both philosophy and politics have tended to be inclusive and pragmatic, rather than exclusive or ethereal. This book is written in that spirit, putting it at odds with some contemporary academic research applied to public policy. In universities different conceptions of how society operates are isolated from each other in separate departments. Standard academic practice is to explain as much as possible by means of the theory of one's own department rather than to acknowledge its limits and the usefulness of other theories. Academic policy research at this point becomes policy *analysis*, taking apart an issue by means of a single discipline. This book is rather an exercise in policy *synthesis*—recognizing the truth and usefulness of different ways of understanding how people act.

A crucial aspect of the argument has to do with the difficulty of establishing the theories underlying public policies. Theories in social science stubbornly resist empirical testing. Anomalies arise that are incompatible with a theory's predictions. Over a century ago Woodrow Wilson alluded to this when he wrote that governing is so difficult because "the people . . . are selfish, ignorant, timid, stubborn, or foolish with the selfishness, the ignorances, the stubbornnesses, the timidities, or the follies of several thousand persons,—albeit there are hundreds who are wise."[9] People are neither all or always mean, nor all or always noble. This book makes the case that in some instances each of those motivations can be dependably channeled toward public purposes. The question is not whether socially productive behavior is *possible*—spontaneous altruism does occur, and evil can serendipitously backfire—but whether it is *dependable*. Two kinds of policies are presented that, under certain circumstances, are dependable. The first, competition, emerges from a new economics of organization, a set of theories that attributes self-interest to individuals, then predicts their behavior. That theory explains much of the inefficiency of government. Competition can oftentimes channel that self-interest to good effect, but there will be times when competition is flawed or impossible. Of course, there will always be the saints or heroes who selflessly and honorably seek to aid the public interest, and whose actions cannot be explained by self-interest theories or the discipline of economics. In the second kind of policy, community, we look out for others, but even so, other-mindedness is not always reliably produced. It must be acknowledged that there will be times when policies resting on these two broad theories will not yield expected results.

Some cautious academicians, recognizing that their theories are imperfect, resist drawing policy inferences when faced with conflicting evidence. But policy must be made. Policymakers must have different standards for judging theories than do those who devise and test them. Decades ago, in a celebrated essay that has greatly influenced social scientists, Milton Friedman argued that a theory is to be judged by its predictions, not its assumptions.[10] To Friedman, if the assumption that people act self-interestedly yields accurate predictions, whether that is, in fact, their motivation is unimportant. To him predictions count, not assumptions. In the social sciences, however, seldom are a theory's predictions sufficiently accurate to render unnecessary the consideration of a competing theory. (Though there will be the thousands who are selfish and ignorant, there will also be the hundreds who are wise.) In that case, the plausibility of the theory itself—the believability of the assumptions and logic that go into its explanation of how people act in given circumstances—becomes a test of whether the theory should be called on to inform policy.

In this book I make a sweeping claim: only two broad types of policy are dependable for the delivery of state government's main services. While there will naturally be exceptions, much of today's policy is actually based on exceptions. Consider the underpinnings, the implicit theories of current policy:

—that increasing government expenditures will tend to yield correspondingly improved outcomes;

—that civil servants are spontaneously public-spirited;

—that providing public employees with better information will ipso facto lead to their using it;

—that legislatures carefully oversee state services;

—that recipients of services from state bureaus have the information and the power to oversee those bureaus and make desired changes.

Those things happen, but not dependably. The arguments for them are simply not plausible. Contemporary social policy lacks mechanisms automatically linking policy and result. Competition and community come as close as possible to providing us with such mechanisms. Current policies lack levers, or theories, that provide a dependable basis for the expectation that the proposed action will lead to the intended result. Legislators frequently come up against the notion that civil servants, especially teachers, can be counted on to seek the public good. They hear this argument because the recipients of current spending are well represented by lobbyists at state capitols. Many legislators, especially Democrats—myself included—want to believe in the nobility of public service. But to the extent that a policy rests on the assumption that by dint of working for government people can be counted on to do good, it is sentimental. People who are offended by that assertion should be prepared to make a plausible claim for why society should expect civil servants regularly to act other-mindedly. Certainly they will, on occasion, but possibility is not plausibility. In our time anyone supporting this or that government policy must bear the burden of making a plausible case for why it should be expected to work. In this book I do just that by arguing in support of the claim that there are only two broad types of policy for delivering state services that are reliable. I will be delighted if, in response, people come up with other dependable, plausible policies.

## An Outline of the Book

Chapter 2 contains a description of what states do, using categories that presage the later argument of the book. This chapter also shows that the states are likely entering a period of difficult fiscal circumstances, much more serious than the situations they have faced in recent decades.

Pervasive failings of state government are described in chapter 3. These failings would not be remedied either by increasing spending or by cutting it. For much of what state governments do there is little relation between spending and results. The budget, commonly and misleadingly called the embodiment of policy, has become a weak instrument.

An explanation for this state of affairs is offered in chapter 4. This chapter's argument is drawn from an economic theory of organization, a theory that has been developing for decades but whose implications have not yet had much effect on the major programs of state government. According to this theory, people, in their public and private dealings, can be expected to act in their own interests, sometimes taking advantage of others as they do so. Organizations—bureaucracy is the prime example—whose members are not systematically influenced by some kind of salutary motivation, reward, or penalty cannot realistically be expected to be socially productive merely by having money allocated to them. Their members are apt to accomplish their private purposes, sometimes slighting the public in the process. Bureaucracy, it need not be emphasized, is state government's standard way of carrying out policy. The inference is drawn that in the future policy-making should involve the design and use of institutions and organizations in which people are methodically oriented to producing desired outcomes, rather than simply allocating a budget among often inefficient organizations.

Chapter 5 presents an array of potential state policies inferred from that critique—ways of carrying out state responsibilities other than through bureaucracy. Those policies, at the heart of which is competition, explicitly use private incentives to harness self-interest to public purposes. That would be an improvement over current practice. But to attempt to construct a comprehensive agenda for the states solely around this idea would soon make clear the limits of the new economics of organization, that is, the limited usefulness of radical individualism as a theory on which to base policy. Self-interest is neither a complete description of human behavior nor a sufficient foundation upon which to build governmental institutions. For society to depend on self-interest alone in designing public policy would be something of a contradiction in terms: if citizens and policymakers only look out for themselves, presumably no one could be expected to design policies in the public interest.

Like James Madison, the main designer of our governmental system, I hold that society needs simultaneously to harness self-interest and to depend on public-spiritedness. Like the Anti-Federalists, the opponents of the Constitution written by Madison and his allies, I believe that public-spiritedness does not necessarily occur spontaneously but must be developed and encouraged.

The idea of community introduced in chapter 6 takes us in a direction different from the approaches advanced in chapter 5. Carrying out some of government's responsibilities through communities, rather than through bureaucracies or firms, offers the opportunity to improve both productivity and esprit de corps. A community is understood here as an organization, membership in which ordinarily draws people to seek the benefit of others. Family and religion are the clearest examples. I recognize the power of policies drawn from economics; there are occasions when such policies can be appropriate and sufficient. However, to ignore the effects of communities on individuals—which economists normally do; for them organizations are only aggregations of autonomous, self-interested individuals—is to be closed to a source of personal fulfillment and societal vigor. Being part of a community can motivate its members to seek to serve the interests of others. There can even be public policy value, supported by evidence of effectiveness, to performing such activities as schooling and providing health care in families, neighborhoods, and religious organizations. Productivity can be enhanced because people in communities spontaneously strive to help one another, and there is less need for the expense of managerial controls. Not only can tax dollars go further, but meeting more of government's responsibilities through communities can actually be more responsive to the wishes of the citizens.

The American way is eclectic, and policymakers have the task of accommodating seemingly conflicting points of view. Only the academician tied to a particular discipline finds it necessary to explain all behavior by means of a single kind of motivation. We are mixtures of motives. A prudent government recognizes our tendency toward self-serving behavior, while simultaneously recognizing and fostering our attempts at other-mindedness. At its core this book acknowledges explanatory and instrumental power in two views, two groups of theories of human motivation. Neither is foolproof, however, and in chapters 4, 5, and 6 as policies of competition and community are justified, the conditions in which they are apt to flounder are also presented.

Chapter 7 contains a menu of policies having the power of choice or community or both. The common thread running through each of these policies is the fact that the people involved are systematically oriented to produce outcomes beneficial to society by being subjected to competition or by membership in a community in which they are bound to others through ties of altruism, meaning love or duty.

The book culminates in chapter 8 with the argument that for most of what government does—the provision of services—it has only these two powerful, largely self-disciplining instruments for meeting societal objectives. Restructuring government comes to be seen as designing these features into policy. Service provision not incorporating at least one of these features needs to be subjected to questioning: why should it be expected that desired results will occur? The admirable efforts of public-spirited bureaucrats, patriotic managers, and charismatic politicians will likely be overwhelmed if the systems in which they work are not supportive of their efforts.

The British statesman David Owen wrote, "The Labor Party has always lacked a theory to explain how the distribution of power was to be altered in order to achieve socialism and how power was to be distributed in a socialist society."[11] This book argues a similar point: the Democratic party—the party of government in the United States—lacks a theory to explain how its aspirations are to be translated into effective action. This fact has been obscured by the occasional good works of politicians and other government workers. But service provision by the states has foundered because of the absence of such a theory. Dependence on universal goodwill among those working for the government and on the automatic efficacy of appropriations can now be recognized as folly. It is not that spending money is futile or that no one working for the government seeks the good of others. Altruistic public service is noble; unfortunately it is hardly commonplace. In contrast with competition and community, current policies—appropriations, exhortations, mandates—lack consistent relationships between the policy and the hoped-for result. Current service provision is inadequate. The defectiveness of current policies puts the burden of defense on them. The case for restructuring of the sort proposed here is not without flaws, but because there are powerful, tested theories behind it, it is stronger than what we have now.

Each of us has a reservoir of talents and abilities and generosity that often is frustrated by our surroundings, especially by the kinds of organizations in which we live and work. The essence of policymaking and creating an agenda for the states lies in redesigning the organizations and institutions through which the states do their work. The problems facing the states are not basically financial or technological. They are cultural, motivational, and organizational. Whether out of concern for economic productivity or for the morale, dignity, and happiness of the American people, the challenge to the states is to restructure the institutions through which they carry out their policies.

An agenda of choice and community is informed by American experience of recent decades as well as by contemporary evaluation research, economics, organization theory, and moral philosophy. It recognizes the implementation of public responsibilities to be crucially important but, as currently done in the states, deeply flawed. It offers a vision of state government that is limited but strong, productive, and satisfying because it draws on the aspirations and talents of citizens.

# 2

# *What State Governments Do Now and Will Do in the Future*

A T THE LAST TURN of a century no one would have predicted the remarkable growth in the size of state governments that has occurred between then and now. For every dollar
expended by the states in 1900 over two thousand dollars are spent
each year in the 1990s. Combining federal aid spent by the states
with the purchases of local governments, which are creatures of
the states, brings annual state spending in the 1990s to nearly one-
fourth of personal income. For all that, federal government spending has grown even faster in this century. When today's elderly
were children, Washington's spending was half that of state and
local governments combined. Now the federal budget exceeds
the sum of the budgets of all subnational governments. All told,
government spending in America has grown from a fourth of personal income in the 1930s to 40 percent in the 1970s and to half in
the 1990s.[1]

## What State Governments Do Now

State spending is hardly limited to the most apparent functions
of educating children and maintaining roads. Anything funded,
produced, or regulated by the national government in Washington has its place in today's state capitols—from veterans' affairs

to economic growth, utility rates to family planning. One purpose of this chapter is to collapse the confusing array of state activities into a few categories in order to better understand the principal role of state government and ways in which it can be improved.[2]

Dollar expenditure is the usual measure of the level and importance of government activity. State functions will be presented in those terms here, though the argument will be made in chapter 3 that spending is an inadequate and misleading gauge of government accomplishment.

Although states are engaged in a myriad of activities, the bulk of their budgets is spent on strikingly few items (see table 2-1). In recent years states have allocated about one-third of their total expenditures to education, one-sixth to medical care, and one-tenth each to social insurance, roads, and welfare (income maintenance and social services for the poor). Those five items alone constitute over three-quarters of all state spending. With the exception of welfare, these are hardly controversial uses of public money, which is to say that there are no large pools of state funds easily shifted to any area thought to be deserving of more money. For a variety of reasons to be discussed shortly, it is most likely that these will continue to be state government's main responsibilities for a long while to come.

Some funds are expended directly by the states, but much more money is transferred to individuals or to the school districts, colleges, municipalities, and county governments that operate the programs on which the money is spent. Indeed, so much of state government spending is allocated to others that it is useful to distinguish between that part of their budgets, just over half, devoted to producing or buying services through the states' own agencies (columns A, B, and C), and that part, just under half, that is devoted not to service production by the states but to income transfer (columns D and E).[3]

Combining columns A and D shows that over half of state budgets is ultimately spent on bureaus. A governmental bureau is an organization funded not by the sale of its products to willing recipients but by lump sum grants from a sponsor (typically a legislature). Its employees cannot legitimately keep the organization's

**Table 2-1. Final Goods and Services and Income Transfers Funded by State Governments, 1990**

Billions of dollars

| | Final goods and services | | | Income transfers | | |
| | State-produced | | State-pur-chased and | To local govern- | To indi- | |
| | Granted[a] | Sold[b] | -granted[c] | ments | viduals | Total |
| | *A* | *B* | *C* | *D* | *E* | |
|---|---|---|---|---|---|---|
| Education | 10 | 67 | * | 103 | 5 | 184 |
| Elementary and secondary | 2 | * | * | 103 | * | 105 |
| Higher | * | 67 | * | * | 5 | 72 |
| Other | 8 | * | * | * | * | 8 |
| Health | 26 | 9 | 56 | 7 | * | 99 |
| Insurance[d] | * | * | * | * | 54 | 54 |
| Transportation | 41 | 3 | * | 10 | * | 54 |
| Welfare | 14 | * | 1 | 22 | 12 | 49 |
| Police, corrections | 20 | * | * | 2 | * | 22 |
| Interest | * | * | * | * | 22 | 22 |
| General admin-istration | 17 | * | * | 1 | * | 18 |
| Natural resources, parks | 10 | 2 | * | 1 | * | 13 |
| Utilities | * | 6 | * | * | 1 | 7 |
| Regulation | 4 | * | * | * | * | 4 |
| Liquor | * | 3 | * | * | * | 3 |
| Other[e] | 18 | 5 | * | 20 | * | 44 |
| Total state expenditures | 160 | 95 | 57 | 166 | 94 | 572 |

Sources: Advisory Commission on Intergovernmental Relations, State-Local Government Finance Diskettes, Washington 1990; and Department of Commerce, *State Government Finance: 1990* (August 1991).

* Less than $500 million.

a. Financing preponderantly from appropriations, not market sales.

b. Financing exclusively (such as utilities) or in significant part (such as higher education tuition and room and board payments) from market sales.

c. Final goods and services purchased by state government from private vendors for granting to and consumption by private individuals.

d. Unemployment compensation, workers' compensation, employee retirement.

e. Includes unrestricted aid to local governments, plus employment services, veterans' services, and aid to libraries.

profits, and they usually are subject to rules stipulating desired behavior.[4]

The organizations producing the items represented in column B receive a sizable part of their revenues from sales to the public; they can be thought of as state-owned enterprises, a cross between bureaus and private firms. Even those organizations bear some of the characteristics of bureaus, however. Typically (as in the case of state colleges), they receive some funding directly from recipients of their services (tuition), while still getting the bulk of their financing in the form of a subsidy from the legislature, as do bureaus.

## Fiscal Prospects for the States

For the foreseeable future, revenues available to the states will grow more slowly than in previous decades. Pressures to spend more on what they are already doing will increase more rapidly than will revenues. Three powerful and persistent forces underlying these observations foretell that the fiscal difficulties of the states will be more serious by the early years of the next century than in recent history. These difficulties make it all but impossible for states to take on major new responsibilities and, at the same time, continue to increase their expenditures at current rates.

### Economic Growth

Even in the prosperous 1990s the American economy is growing more slowly than it did for the previous several decades. Though there was considerable annual variation from 1960 to 1990, gross domestic product grew by just over 3 percent a year during that period after adjusting for inflation.[5] Even optimistic looks into the future yield projections short of that rate. The U.S. Bureau of Labor Statistics projects annual growth of 2.2 percent through the year 2005 (with a low-growth possibility of 1.5 percent and a high-growth possibility of 3.0 percent).[6] Even if the federal government adopts a balanced budget policy, the Congressional Budget Office, the Clinton administration, and the consensus of American economists represented by Blue Chip Economic Indicators all project growth of 2.2 to 2.3 percent a year from the late 1990s through the first half-dozen years of the next decade.[7] Two enduring factors contribute to this sobering expectation. The number of new workers entering the labor force has decreased in the 1990s and will continue to do so in the 2000s, and labor force productivity (that is, output per worker) in the 1990s is maintaining the slower rate of the 1980s, rather than the rapid rate of the 1950s and 1960s.

In the 1990s the proportion of adults in the labor force has grown to two-thirds, the highest level ever.[8] Not only has the baby boom generation come of age, but unprecedentedly large increases have occurred in the number of women in the work force. In recent decades, with relatively slow wage growth and correspondingly small increases in family earnings, millions of women turned for the first time to work for pay and thus increased the income of their households. From 1970 to the mid-1990s the proportion of white women in the labor force grew from barely 40 percent to nearly 60 percent. This phenomenon could happen but once. Whereas from 1975 to 1990 the labor force grew by 1.9 percent a year, from 1990 to 2005 it will grow by only 1.3 percent annually. Thereafter growth will be slower yet. In the near term the non-working population of the United States will be growing nearly as fast as the working population; the baby boom generation will start to reach retirement age and the boomlet of births to the children of the baby boomers will continue. In the 1990s and the first decade of the next century the dependency ratio (the number of persons outside the labor force divided by the number in it) will decline only slowly; after 2010 it will actually rise, rapidly, as the baby boomers retire.[9]

In comparison with the recent past, only small future increases in personal income will come from there being a larger proportion of the population working, and that will happen only through the first decade of the new century. For a generation or more thereafter, an ever smaller fraction of the population will be in the work force.[10] To have enhanced prosperity the country will have to depend on large improvements in productivity, that is, in output per worker.

**Table 2-2. Annual Growth in U.S. Output per Worker, 1950–2005**

Percent

|           |         |
|-----------|---------|
| 1950–64   | 2.7     |
| 1965–73   | 1.8     |
| 1974–80   | 0.6     |
| 1981–88   | 1.3     |
| 1990–2005 | 1.3–1.4 |

Sources: D. W. Rasmussen and I. Kim, "The Growth of U.S. Labour Productivity 1950–1989," *Applied Economics,* vol. 24 (March 1992), p. 286; and Norman C. Saunders, "The U.S. Economy into the 21st Century," in Bureau of Labor Statistics, "Outlook: 1990–2005" (Department of Labor, 1992).

Unfortunately, there is little indication that the American work force is becoming appreciably more productive. In the two decades following World War II output per worker grew by over 2½ percent per year (see table 2-2). Thereafter, labor productivity grew slowly in the late 1960s and early 1970s (partly because of the shock to the economy from large increases in oil prices, making inefficient many parts of the economy that had been predicated on cheap fuel), and proceeded to grow hardly at all in the mid- and late 1970s. Productivity growth in the 1980s still lagged far behind that of the immediate postwar decades. From the vantage point of the 1990s, it appears that the high growth rates of the 1950s and 1960s were exceptional.[11] A backlog of ideas ripe for commercial use had developed during the Great Depression and World War II. Their application in the immediate postwar period yielded productivity improvement in the United States at rates that then dropped and have remained considerably lower ever since.

As the economy grows slowly—and even if it were to start growing faster—it will be difficult for the states to extract appreciably more taxes from their citizens. In recent decades, when the economy was growing faster than appears likely for the foreseeable future, the fraction of personal income going to state and local taxes and fees rose from 13.1 percent in 1970, to 13.3 percent in 1980, 14.8 percent in 1985, 15.2 percent in 1990, and 15.4 percent in 1992.[12] The tax protests of the 1990s suggest that in the future there will be little popular enthusiasm to pay the states and localities an even higher fraction of slower-growing incomes.

### *Demographic Influences on the Demand for State Services*

The number of recipients of the states' largest entitlement programs is growing more rapidly than in the past, and within that group the number with a claim on the most expensive services is growing fastest.

Throughout much of the 1970s and 1980s elementary and secondary school enrollments fell. They have risen in the 1990s and will continue upward into the new century. (By 2015 it is expected that the annual number of births in the United States will exceed the highest levels of the baby boom years.) The number of high school students dropped by 2.0 million in the 1980s and has risen by 1.7 million in the 1990s. The proportion of Latinos and African Americans in the schools is growing rapidly. In the 1990s, two-thirds of all school children are white. By the turn of the century that fraction will shrink slightly for the high schools. But dramatic changes are occurring in the elementary schools. In the 1990s the number of white students in elementary school has remained steady. Most of the 4 million increase in five- to fourteen-year-olds during the decade will be made up of Latino and African American children. The number of Latino elementary-age children will grow by nearly one-third in that period; the number of African Americans by more than one-sixth. (In 1995 the number of Latinos added to the American population surpassed the number of additional non-Latino whites; by 2005 the same will start occurring for African Americans.)[13] Assuring equal educational opportunities to the growing number of children of color will be more difficult than educating their white contemporaries. The vast majority of African American children are now born and raised outside marriage, while the illegitimacy rate for whites has passed one-fifth and is rising.[14] A national survey of young people found that high school children being raised in a single-parent family are twice as likely to use drugs and half again as likely to be depressed, to have attempted suicide, to have engaged in vandalism, and to have been in trouble with the police. Furthermore, "at risk differences between youth in single- and two-parent families persist even after race and . . . levels of maternal education, which is a reasonable proxy for family income . . . are taken into account."[15] Children without a father present in their lives have a higher incidence of learning and psychological disorders and go on to commit a hugely disproportionate number of the nation's crimes.[16] Like other problems of youth, the "relationship between crime and one-parent families" is "so strong that controlling for family configuration erases the relationship between race and crime and between low income and crime."[17] Sara McLanahan and Gary Sandefur find the situation to be even more grim than that, saying, "Children who grow up in a household with only one biological parent are worse off, on average, than children who grow up in a household with both of their biological parents, regardless of the parents' race or educational background, regardless of whether the parents are married when the child is born, and regardless of whether the resident parent remarries."[18] To overcome the conditions in which most minority children and a growing number of other American youngsters find themselves will require heroic and sometimes expensive efforts. That suggests spending pressure on government.[19]

In a 1994 study, the Rand Corporation found encouraging relationships among race, family characteristics, and student achievement. While noting that on average, African American children score about 0.7 standard deviations lower than whites on achievement tests (the Latino-white gap is slightly smaller), the Rand researchers found that remarkable improvement in student achievement and some family characteristics of nonwhite children had taken place in the 1980s. Within that population, parental education rose and the number of children per family fell. Both of these changes seem to be associated positively with academic achievement. Surprisingly, they also found that "the direct effects on achievement are very small from increased numbers of single-parent families," meaning that, by itself, single parenthood might have little adverse effect on a child's achievement.[20] Still, the increase in student numbers in the 1990s is taking place almost entirely in populations such as African Americans and Latinos where the demographic factors associated with student achievement—income, family size, presence of father in home, mother's education, father's education, mother's age at birth—all are unfavorable by comparison with white children. There has been improvement in some of those categories among the nonwhite population, followed by a considerable narrowing of the achievement gap between nonwhites and whites. However, on average, whites are still advantaged in every one of these regards. For years to come students, as a group, will constitute a much more daunting educational challenge for society than in the past.

Paying for the education of these children will be difficult. In the 1970s and 1980s, when school enrollments were declining and the number of persons earning incomes was rising rapidly, it was relatively easy for the states to spend more tax money *per child.* But in the foreseeable future, with rising numbers of students and a slower growing economy, significant per student expenditure increases such as the schools have been receiving will be most unlikely.

In health care, state government's next largest expenditure category, demographic trends also foretell spending pressures. The number of persons over 65, where health care expenditures are concentrated, will grow slowly until a decade or so into the new century. Thereafter, as we have seen, the baby boom generation will start to move into retirement. But the fastest growing segment among the aged—indeed, among the entire population—is, and for many decades into the future will be, those over 85 years of age. In the three decades following 1990, that group will double in size, growing five times as fast as the population as a whole. Under current policies more and more of those people seem destined to live in nursing homes. By the time of their death the room, board, and medical care of many nursing home residents are covered by medicaid, a program jointly funded by Washington and the states.[21] In the mid-1990s government health care expenditures were rising more slowly than in previous years as nearly full employment and efforts to reduce the welfare rolls cut the rate of increase in eligible persons. Still, government's spending on health care can be expected to continue to grow at rates far greater than the growth in the economy and tax revenues.[22]

Corrections, though a much smaller part of state budgets than education or health, is the fastest growing of all state government activities. From 1970 to 1990, while the population of the country grew by 23 percent, the number of prisoners in state correctional facilities nearly quadrupled, rising from 176,000 to 690,000, an increase of 292 percent, or 7 percent a year. In the 1980s and early 1990s, the number of state prisoners was growing still faster, by over 8 percent a year, far exceeding the percentage increases in population, national output, and tax revenue.[23] If that rate continues, the population of state prisons would quadruple again in less than eighteen years.

Elementary and secondary education, health, and corrections take four dollars of every ten spent by the states, and that proportion is growing rapidly. In all three of those areas the demography of the country is adding greatly increased numbers of people for whom the programs tend to be very expensive. In California, if present demographic and spending trends in these three areas continue, there will be almost no money at all left for higher education or anything else by as early as the first years of the next century.[24] Even in relatively well-off Minnesota, just maintaining real per capita expenditures at their current levels in those three areas would create a succession of budget deficits in the mid-2000s requiring the equivalent of eliminating the prison system, the community college system, or special education every two years for the indefinite future.[25]

### Prospects for Federal Aid to the States

Attempts to balance the federal budget will exacerbate the fiscal difficulties of the states. As a fraction of total state and local spending, federal financial assistance reached a peak in 1978. In that year 26.5 percent of state and local expenditures were covered by Washington. By the 1990s only about 20 percent of state and local expenditures were paid by the federal government, and the composition of the aid had changed considerably. In the 1970s, one in six dollars of federal aid went to health care; in the 1990s the proportion has risen to two in five.[26] Although that ratio could reach half by the turn of the century, this large increase in health care aid does not release state funds for spending elsewhere. Health care aid is almost entirely granted to the states under the medicaid program, which requires a match that varies by state up to the amount received from Washington.

The increase is explained, of course, by the rapid rise in medical care costs plus the increase in the number of recipients of medicaid. Meanwhile, except for income maintenance programs, notably aid to families with dependent children, which in 1996 was abolished and pushed off to the states, the portion of federal aid devoted to all other purposes dropped in the 1980s and 1990s. Federal funding (adjusted for inflation) for education, the environment, and nearly every other major object of aid, with the exception of health and welfare, has been lower in the 1990s than in the 1980s.[27]

Now, might that turn around? Might federal aid in the future bail out the states? No! The same slower-moving economy from which worried state policymakers draw their tax revenues faces the federal government. Of overriding importance has been the federal budget deficit. In the two decades following 1970, federal taxes stood at 23 to 25 percent of personal income. However, in that period expenditures rose by about 4 percent of personal income. The difference was the deficit. The accumulated deficit is the debt, interest on which crowds out other federal expenditures. As recently as the mid-1970s, the federal government spent twice as much money on aid to the states and localities as on interest payments. In the 1990s, annual interest payments have exceeded total aid to the states.[28] Balancing the federal budget will wreak havoc on state budgets, for even when the federal budget comes into balance immense interest payments will continue to make other expenditures more difficult.

As the federal government restrains its spending in order to cut its deficit, the fiscal exigencies of the states will be intensified in several ways. By the early part of the new century, aid to the states is apt to be about 25 percent lower than would be the case under existing law, a decrease that could be upwards of $67 billion (in 1995 dollars) annually.[29] How much is $67 billion? It is more than all the states and localities combined spend on police and fire protection, more than the sum of their spending on corrections, natural resources and parks.[30] Beneficiaries of federal aid programs will expect the states to make up for federal cuts. Meanwhile, if the federal government were to resort to increasing taxes, state tax increases would become all the more difficult to enact. States and localities were able to raise taxes and fees from 13 percent of personal income in 1980 to 15 percent in 1990 partly because the federal government, to a great extent, was borrowing instead of taxing during that period.[31] Even before the federal government started seriously tackling its deficit, federal policy had already made state taxing more onerous. Deductibility of state taxes from income for federal tax purposes has long made state taxes considerably less burdensome than they would otherwise be. When state sales taxes were deductible on the federal income tax form, and the highest federal marginal income tax rates exceeded 50 percent, the "tax price," that is, the net cost to a state taxpayer, was, for many people, less than fifty cents for each dollar collected by state government. But, in the 1980s, the federal government made state taxes more expensive when it ended the deductibility of state sales taxes and reduced the marginal rates on the federal income tax.

## Conclusion

State government spending is divided roughly evenly between the provision of services and transfers of income. Each of those categories is dominated by a handful of items, almost all of which are widely accepted as appropriate state responsibilities by citizens. There are no large unpopular objects of expenditure from which funds could be easily shifted in order to expand appropriations for a favored program.

The states are entering a period of very stringent finances. Interest groups seeking more funds for their programs will suppose that money will come to them from somewhere. But all of the large state expenditure categories will be under demographic pressure for spending increases. This will be in an era of slower economic growth and a time when state tax increases have been made even more difficult by federal policy. Finally, federal budget policy will only make things more painful for state governments.

The states have gone through a period of remarkable growth in real per capita expenditures for their major responsibilities. That period is about to come to an end.

# 3

## Do State Taxpayers Get Their Money's Worth?

THE MOST IMPORTANT finding of policy evaluation in recent decades is simple: for much of what government does, little relationship exists between the amount of money spent and the results achieved. Though some government activities are regularly more effective than others, the great increases in state spending have not produced corresponding effects. More money does not mean more impact. This chapter is devoted to that unsettling situation, and to distinguishing between those state policies in which expenditures do not ordinarily translate into desired results and those that do better.

A government's budget is often said to be the manifestation of its policy. The late political scientist Aaron Wildavsky, the country's most eminent student of budgeting, called budgeting "the major issue of American politics."[1] "Public budgets," says Irene Rubin in the first sentence of *The Politics of Public Budgeting*, "describe what governments do by listing how governments spend money."[2] Economists like to think of decisionmaking in general as the allocation of scarce resources, budgeting being the most obvious example. And few legislators decline an opportunity for appointment to the appropriations committee. That's where the money is.

Those who study budgets or decide on them are not the only ones who see policymaking as the determination of who gets how much money. The recipients think that way too. They, or their lobbyists, encourage all to perceive a budget increase as the way society expresses its concern about an issue. Reducing expenditure on an item is, in the words of budgeting's favorite cliche, "balancing the budget on the backs of" the affected group.

But understanding the essence of policymaking to be allocating money diverts attention from whether spending accomplishes results. If spending money does not generally translate into achievements, then policymaking must involve more than the distribution of funds. Recall that over half of state spending now consists of direct or indirect subsidies to public bureaus that produce services granted to individuals. Elementary and secondary education is the archetype, and will serve to investigate the relationship between expenditures and accomplishments. The schooling of children makes a good example not only because more than one dollar in every six spent by the states goes to it, but because there has been much illuminating research on whether spending money on schooling yields well-educated youngsters. Furthermore, education attracts idealistic, motivated workers—teachers— eager to be of service. If funds spent there do not bring about corresponding results, how likely is it that other state bureaucracies, whose workers might have less inspiring missions, will excel at putting their resources to productive use?

## The Dismal Record of Elementary and Secondary Education

Americans are becoming accustomed to hearing that their children are ill educated, but the facts still hit harshly. The federal government's National Assessment of Educational Progress regularly gauges the educational achievement of the nation's youth. NAEP finds that *most* seventeen-year-olds lack "any degree of detailed knowledge across the subdisciplines of science," lack "an overall understanding of specific government structures and their functions," and lack knowledge of some of the most basic historical facts. Fewer than half are familiar with the Declaration of Independence; half are unaware that the Constitution guarantees freedom of religion. Most don't know about the mid-nineteenth-century debate on slavery, nor can they tell you about Martin Luther King Jr. and the Montgomery boycott. Half think that a boat trip from New York to London is as benefited by the Panama Canal as is a voyage from New York to San Francisco. One-third of our high school seniors cannot write a persuasive letter, and a third do not know that we have a representative democracy or what separation of powers means. Half of American eleventh graders are studying either pre–high school mathematics or none at all; only half of our seventeen-year-olds can do grade school mathematics (decimals, fractions, percents, and simple equations). Three in a hundred of our secondary school students study calculus; five times that many do so in Japan, where a higher proportion of young people graduate than do here. This all leaves nearly half of our seventeen-year-olds lacking the reading and mathematics skills required to be hired for work in an automobile manufacturing plant. By the end of their high school years U.S. students rank low in international comparisons of academic achievement.[3]

One rejoinder to this sorry litany is that surely we would do better if only we would increase appropriations going to education. But just that has been happening for decades. In barely a generation, the third of a century between 1960 and 1990, per student spending on elementary and secondary education in the United States, in 1990 dollars, rose from $1,621 to $4,960.[4] That means, after adjusting for inflation, three times as many resources are devoted to the schooling of the average pupil of the 1990s as were spent on that child's parents when they were in school a generation earlier.[5] Now, can it be that children a few decades ago learned a third as much, having had only a third as much money spent on them? Hardly. For most of that period results of standardized achievement tests dropped before beginning a rise that leaves average scores in the 1990s about where they were in the 1960s.[6]

To investigate the influence educational expenditures exert on educational outcomes, Eric Hanushek assembled 187 studies that examined this relationship. He concluded not only that there is "no strong evidence that teacher-student ratios, teacher education, or teacher experience have the expected positive effects on student achievement," but that in general, "there is no strong or systematic relationship between school expenditures and student performance."[7] The Hanushek finding has been lamented and excoriated, but not persuasively refuted. Various researchers have criticized Hanushek, citing instances in which money has made a difference.[8] That, however, is not in dispute. The grievous fact remains that, on average, the enormous increases in spending on schools in recent decades have not yielded corresponding improvements in educational outcomes.

## Spending on Schools Can Make a Difference

It is important that the point made above not be misunderstood. No one is arguing that additional expenditures cannot yield better-educated students. There are many schools in which they do. But the sequence of money producing expected results is neither automatic nor even common. Simply spending more money is not sufficient.

In the 1970s and 1980s a body of research grew up under the name of the Effective Schools Movement. Scholars had noticed that although, on average, there were trifling educational improvements when expenditures increased, the average represented a distribution of positive and negative results. They set out to determine what was different about the more successful schools and found in them strong leadership, an orderly environment, the teaching of basic skills, high expectations of students, homework regularly assigned and accomplished, a substantial part of the students' day spent on academic work, systematic monitoring of students' progress, and a sense on the part of students, teachers, and parents that their school is a community.[9]

More recently, researchers have discovered other signs of improved educational outcomes. Researchers have identified a very significant narrowing of the gap in educational achievement between African American and white students in the United States.[10] In the 1970s and 1980s, about half of that gap in reading achievement was eliminated, as were 25 to 40 percent (depending on the age of the groups compared) of the mathematics gap and 15 to 25 percent of the science gap. By the end of the 1980s the gap had narrowed because African American levels improved; white achievement levels were no higher than they had been twenty years earlier.[11] The identified reasons for this development have mostly to do with the relative increase in years of schooling of African American parents, the increased opportunity to attend nursery school, and especially the relative decline in poverty among African Americans. (Some have surmised that perhaps federal programs targeted to minority youth have had beneficial results, a hypothesis that deserves testing.) However, in the 1990s, despite continued increases in education spending on both African Americans and whites, poverty levels among both groups have risen and the achievement gap between them may no longer be narrowing.[12]

More useful signs of school resources yielding increased student achievement have emerged. Ronald Ferguson found that, in Texas, students perform better if their teachers possess strong language skills, many years of experience, or a master's degree, a finding at odds with Hanushek's and all the more significant since Ferguson determined that disparities in educational achievement translate later into differentials in earnings.[13] Others have discerned "a strong relationship between school quality and the economic returns to additional years of schooling for black and white workers."[14]

The most elegant study that finds a favorable effect of spending on educational results is that of Ronald Ferguson and Helen Ladd.[15] They concluded that, in Alabama, teacher quality and class size significantly influence learning achieved by students. Even though that finding flies in the face of the research that detects little relationship between spending and results on average, a plausible reconciliation of the two bodies of research exists: additional funds applied to a low-spending school (for example, in Alabama) have greater effect than if applied to a high-spending school. Also, though teacher quality has been shown to contribute to positive student outcomes, higher pay does not necessarily yield better teachers. The one ambitious attempt to determine the relationship in the United States between teacher pay and the quality of teachers found that "higher teacher salaries have had little if any discernible impact on the quality of newly recruited teachers." This stands to reason, for as Dale Ballou and Michael Podgursky found, "teacher salaries are not differentiated on the basis of performance," and "recruitment of better teachers is further impeded by the fact that public schools show no preference for applicants who have strong academic records."[16]

The finding that under certain circumstances spending matters is not difficult to understand. One might expect that Ferguson and Ladd and the Effective Schools Movement would quickly have been heeded, in the sense that school boards and administrators would create more orderly environments and hire teachers facile with language, and that teachers would assign homework and hold children to higher standards. Unfortunately, evidence of their effectiveness has not led to widespread adoption of those homely practices. By and large, the continually increasing funds being spent on schooling have not been dedicated to uses known to have beneficial effect. The money is being devoted rather to higher teacher salaries and lower class sizes, neither of which, on average, has been strongly related to student achievement.[17] In the post–World War II era teachers have attained a comfortable standard of living (which could hardly be held against them), and the average class size in the United States has dropped from 27 to 17.[18] (In the beginning of this century average class size was 37.)[19] Meanwhile, the education level of American youngsters has become a national disgrace. If class size matters, it certainly doesn't matter enough.

In recent decades schools have taken on a variety of functions not previously their responsibility—for example, social services for troubled families, contraceptive counseling, and police protection. It might be argued that the costs of education are distorted and exaggerated by including money spent on those items. But, the point is that those efforts and their contribution to the tripling of real per student expenditures in thirty years have not been sufficient to overcome the social problems at which they were directed. Educational outcomes remain unsatisfactory. Current social, political, and educational arrangements do not accomplish acceptable education of our children.

This fact, combined with the fiscal prospects of the states, tells us that there is no practical possibility for the foreseeable future that the schools, as currently organized, could receive enough additional money to produce substantial improvements. *Tripling* real expenditures in a generation was not a sufficient budgetary increase. What would it take, say, to *double* real education expenditures again? Well, the number of elementary and secondary students in the United States is growing by about 1 percent a year.[20] Doubling the real expenditures per student would be accomplished in a decade by increasing total, inflation-adjusted, precollegiate education spending by 8 percent annually for each of those ten years. That is not going to happen. The education system has grown accustomed to large budget increases per student, but for a long while to come the states will find it exceedingly difficult to keep real expenditures per student constant.

Budget increases have not typically yielded corresponding improvements in elementary and secondary educational outcomes in the past, and if education in America improves in the future, large amounts of additional money will not be what does it.

## The Inefficacy of Other State-Funded Bureaus

The inadequate record of schooling in America is troubling in its own right, but highlighting it here has the purpose, as well, of illustrating the general problems with production of services by contemporary state and local government bureaus. We have seen that while elementary and secondary education consumes about one-sixth of spending by the states, an additional two-fifths of their budgets goes to other state and local government bureaus. Measurements detailing the inefficacy of that spending are less abundant than are those for elementary and secondary education. Evidence of bureaucratic inefficiency is mostly comparative, showing that some government bureaus spend hugely more than others that are doing the same thing. Those differences are greater than the average difference in efficiency between government bureaus and private firms.

The most sophisticated attempts to determine whether higher-cost bureaus yield correspondingly greater results than those spending less money have been those of the Manpower Demonstration Research Corporation. Daniel Friedlander and Judith M. Gueron of the MDRC report on a series of experiments designed to determine the effectiveness of programs for moving people from welfare to work for pay. They summarize the results of thirteen such experiments involving 68,000 people. Friedlander and Gueron conclude that the "existing experimental research indicates that both the lowest- and highest-cost programs can have lasting effects." However, as to whether on average, higher spending programs yield greater results than lower spending programs, the MDRC concludes that "this question cannot be answered definitely at this time."[21]

Other less rigorous studies come to a similar conclusion. Barbara Stevens found very large differences between local governments in their costs of producing a variety of services: "over 400 percent in payroll, . . . over 700 percent in janitorial services, . . . almost 600 percent in street sweeping, . . . 350 percent in refuse collection, . . . over 300 percent for traffic signal maintenance, . . . 450 percent for asphalt overlay, . . . almost 500 percent for turf maintenance, . . . and over 600 percent in street tree maintenance."[22] When some governments spend four or five or eight times as much money to accomplish a given service as other governments do, notwithstanding that quality has not been controlled for, there is considerable inefficiency to explain.

Not only do some government bureaus often operate inefficiently by comparison with the bureaus of other governments, but private firms have been found to produce many services at lower cost than governments. Table 3-1 shows average amounts by which private costs of producing a variety of services are less than public costs of doing the same thing. The references listed there are themselves compendiums of other studies, so the table reflects dozens of comparisons of public and private costs.

An occasional study of a particular service, for example garbage collection or payroll preparation, shows no difference in cost between public bureaus and private firms. In general, however, for those and other services, sizable cost differences persist between public and private production. But that is not the central point here. Comparing the data in table 3-1 with Stevens's find-

**Table 3-1. Reported Differences between Public and Private Costs for Production of Services[a]**

Percent

| Study | Solid waste | Road construction and maintenance | Libraries | Urban buses | In-patient mental health | General municipal services | Parks | Transportation |
|---|---|---|---|---|---|---|---|---|
| Clarkson | 22–30 | 25–50 | . . . | 20–60 | 10–40 | 30–47 | 14–38 | 30 |
| Bennett and Johnson | 0–59 | . . . | . . . | . . . | . . . | 31–47 | . . . | . . . |
| Stevens | 30 | 30–49 | . . . | . . . | . . . | 0–42 | . . . | . . . |
| Silkman and Young | . . . | . . . | 69 | . . . | . . . | . . . | . . . | 53 |

a. Percentages are amounts by which private costs are lower than public.

Sources: Kenneth W. Clarkson, "Privatization at the State and Local Level," in Paul W. MacAvoy and others, eds., *Privatization and State-Owned Enterprises: Lesson from the United States, Great Britain and Canada* (Boston: Kluwer Academic Publishers, 1989), pp. 143–94; James T. Bennett and Manuel H. Johnson, "Tax Reduction without Sacrifice: Private-Sector Production of Public Services," *Public Finance Quarterly*, vol. 8 (October 1980), pp. 363–96; Barbara J. Stevens, "Comparing Public- and Private-Sector Productive Efficiency: An Analysis of Eight Activities," *National Productivity Review*, vol. 3 (Autumn 1984), pp. 395–406; and Richard Silkman and Dennis R. Young, "X-Efficiency and State Formula Grants," *National Tax Journal*, vol. 35 (September 1982), pp. 383–97.

ings shows that cost differences within government are an order of magnitude greater than those between government and private production. We conclude that in some governments there are large inefficiencies that some other governments and private firms have shown to be remediable.

On the average, state-funded bureaus show little relation between dollars spent on them and results achieved. In some situations there is adequate, even stellar, performance. Research has identified a number of those instances of unusual effectiveness and even what it is that distinguishes them from less productive activities. Catalogs of effective approaches have been published.[23] The Ford Foundation and the John F. Kennedy School of Government at Harvard University team up each year to grant large awards to state and local governments for innovative projects supposedly easy to replicate. More significant than those innovations, however, is their rarity. What is widely known to be effective does not characterize what is generally done in practice.

Elementary and secondary education is representative of the bureaus on which state governments spend most of their money: spending is generous; much is known about how to improve results; what is known is not done; and public expectations are not met. As state policy is currently carried out in bureaus, differences in outcomes are very great and are not explained by budget allocation.

## The Record of State Government Enterprises

Intermediate between government bureaus and private firms are state-owned enterprises (column B of table 2-1). These are agencies that receive a sizable portion of their revenues from sales of their products and that, to some extent, must compete with other entities to make those sales.[24] (In contrast, bureaus are funded not by sales but by lump sum transfers from legislative bodies and are usually monopolies or nearly so—an example of this is the public school system.) As we saw earlier, one state dollar in six is spent on enterprises; more than two-thirds of this spending is directed to postsecondary education. (Some of the things states sell besides higher education are: products of government-owned public utilities, medical care to certain residents of state institutions, admission to parks, and even liquor.) After a brief summary of the overall record of government enterprises we will consider the effectiveness of public colleges and universities, which in the United States are almost all sponsored by state governments.

Over the years scores of studies of the efficiency of government enterprises have been conducted. Generally they have produced more nuanced findings than has research on bureaus: there is greater efficiency in those public enterprises that are subject to competition, and usually only small differences stand out between the efficiency of public and private entities, with private enterprises more often found to outperform public than the other way around. An occasional study of electric utilities, water delivery, or nursing homes finds public enterprises outperforming private, but in those and all other areas (such as refuse collection, airlines, and transit) except railroads most studies find private enterprises to be somewhat more efficient.[25]

For state budgets overall, one dollar in eight goes to higher education, almost all directed to public institutions (though some states devote a small part of their higher education budget to loan and grant programs for students attending private institutions). But unlike elementary and secondary education, public colleges and universities in the United States receive only partial funding from government. Tuition at public higher education institutions can be understood as a price that typically covers one-fourth to two-fifths of the cost of instruction. The balance is picked up by state governments through their appropriations to the institutions. Room and board on campus is paid directly by the student.

In the early 1990s, about 11 million students were enrolled in public higher education institutions and 3 million in private. In the 1980s, the number of students attending public colleges and universities held steady at about 78 percent and has continued at that level through the 1990s. (By comparison, just short of 90 percent of elementary and secondary students are enrolled in public schools.) On average, public institutions are much larger than private; though nearly four-fifths of all higher education students are enrolled in public institutions, there are more private colleges and universities than public in America.[26]

Unlike the case of elementary and secondary education, there have been few attempts to measure the relationship between money spent and results achieved in higher education. The most ambitious such study, by Jeffrey Gilmore, then of the U.S. Department of Education, was limited to estimating this relationship for private institutions. Gilmore concluded that "in general, consumers can indeed judge an institution's quality by its price, [but] there are wide ranges of performance in each price category. That is, while most higher-priced colleges do better than most lower-priced institutions, some low-cost colleges outperform even the most expensive schools."[27] That conclusion, tempered though it is, suggests a stronger relationship between spending and quality in higher education than is the case for elementary and secondary education.

A similar survey has not been done for public institutions, but two indirect measures bolster the claim for that stronger relationship holding there as well. The first of these is the personal and societal payoff from postsecondary education. Charles Clotfelter has estimated the returns to college education by comparing earnings (net of out-of-pocket and opportunity costs) of college graduates with earnings of high school graduates who have not attended college.[28] His calculations suffer from his not having attempted to separate out that part of the income differential due to ability differences and to other factors not having to do with college.[29] (He does note a countervailing factor: "If college increases the nonmarket incomes of graduates, the calculated returns will be understated.") Clotfelter finds both that for individuals, returns to college education are sizable (9.6 percent in 1987 for men, 8.5 percent for women), and, after falling in the 1970s, the returns have since been rising.[30] Those returns to individual students are larger than the returns he calculates for the whole of society (9.1 percent and 7.8 percent), reflecting the fact that most students receive large subsidies from the rest of society when they pay tuition that covers only a small fraction of the cost of their instruction.[31] Clotfelter's estimates indicate that on average a college education is financially worthwhile for an individual and for the whole of society. This conclusion is consistent with Gilmore's finding. That is, some students encounter lower costs and some receive higher returns for the money spent on them than do others, but overall the investment is worthwhile.

There is another, simple but persuasive, argument that spending in higher education is more closely associated with outcomes than is the case for elementary and secondary education. Even though enrollments have been rising in America, one in three higher education institutions lost students in the 1990s. "The marketplace . . . imposes its discipline. Institutions that do not deliver services that a sufficient number of students find attractive must change course or suffer decline."[32]

## State Grants to Local Governments

Nearly half of state spending goes not to direct production of goods and services but to income transfers to local governments (29 percent of all state expenditures) or to individuals (16 percent). Most of the redistribution to local governments is to school districts, and the remainder goes to cities, counties, and townships and their property tax payers. I will investigate below the extent to which state aid has been distributed in defensible fashion. Presumably giving money away is easier than performing services, so in this realm one might expect the states to have a more creditable record.

### School Aid

In the American states except for Hawaii, public education has always been locally organized. Even today more funding for elementary and secondary schools is raised locally than comes from either the state capitals or Washington.[33] (Hawaii has a state-operated system and unlike other states is not subdivided into locally governed districts.) School districts raise funds by levying a property tax. Most states have a constitutional mandate to provide public education, and typically state constitutions stipulate that schooling opportunities should be uniform.[34]

A century ago when states started subsidizing local schools they ordinarily did so by making equal per student grants. In this century, the standard form of aid became the foundation system whereby the state guarantees a minimum, or foundation spending level per child, imposes a standard rate of property taxation statewide, and in each district makes up from state monies the difference between the foundation amount and what is raised locally by application of the statewide rate. Across the country, the foundation amounts have tended to be low, however, and districts wealthy in property have found it easier than have property-poor districts to supplement spending by levying additional local taxes.

Dissatisfaction with the meager amount of redistribution accomplished, specifically with the funds available to poor districts, led to a spate of lawsuits in the 1970s, 1980s, and 1990s. These, in turn, engendered intense debate over what constitutes equity in funding and even over what constitutes equality. In recent years one-third of the states have turned in some measure to "power equalizing" as a device for supplementing foundation aid. Under power equalization, the state in effect makes available to each school district the same tax base per student. Each local district then decides its rate of taxation. The "power" of the property tax— the amount of money per student made available by any given tax rate—is the same for each district because the state supplements the amount raised in a poor district and, possibly, recovers for redistribution elsewhere some of the taxes levied by wealthy districts. For several reasons even the introduction of power equalizing has left considerable unease over the variation in amount spent across districts within states. One reason is that no state actually recovers funds from wealthy districts for use elsewhere, so nowhere has power equalization been fully implemented. The power of a tax rate remains stronger in affluent districts. (Wisconsin and Texas have even been prevented by state courts from accomplishing recovery.) Although under power equalizing poorer districts have the capacity to set high rates and thus bring in large amounts of state aid, in practice they tend to set rates lower than do wealthier districts. Making the opportunity for equal funding available to all districts has not resulted in local choices that in fact accomplish equal funding.

Perhaps the most vexing issue complicating the effort to equalize education funding is the fact that some children, by reason of discrimination, family hardship, or physical handicap are harder to educate than are others. It can be argued that equality requires greater expenditure on such children.

Some researchers have conjectured that increases in spending on the schooling of African American youngsters have brought about some improvement in results.[35] Still, as we have seen, the overall results are disappointing and the prospects bleak. An attempt to measure recent changes in the amount of redistribution accomplished by state policies of school aid concludes that in the 1980s there was little reduction in the variation of education spending across districts within states. In only two-thirds of the states was there movement toward greater equality of education spending in 1987 than in 1980.[36]

## Aid to Cities, Counties, and Individual Property Tax Payers

The scant available evidence suggests that state aid to cities and counties accomplishes even less redistribution than that to school districts. In the 1970s, with Minnesota leading the way, in response to the protests of local property tax payers many states increased state income and sales taxes and used the funds to provide property tax relief both directly to individuals and in the form of aid to local governments. Thus did redistribution of funds grow to become nearly half of state spending. I became a legislator after a huge fiscal recycling system was in place and would guess that those who had designed it had not fully appreciated the logrolling snarls they were creating. As an assistant majority leader and as a tax committee vice chairman I was frequently in a position of having to twist arms or adjust legislation in order to garner a majority of votes for a bill. A large system of aid to local governments is an invitation to a legislator to withhold one's vote until cities in one's district receive more aid. Something of a tradition has arisen in the Minnesota legislature (and I am sure, elsewhere) for each member not to vote for the annual bill that contains adjustments to local government aid until it includes funds to crow about back home. A few years ago a group of researchers led by Helen Ladd studied the property tax relief system in Minnesota. They found that the correlation coefficient between state aid received by a city, and its need as measured by Ladd and her colleagues, was 0.1.[37] That result is only marginally better than would have occurred if the money had been strewn about the state from an airplane. A similarly slight relationship was found by John Yinger when he studied Nebraska and found that "current state aid programs offset about 8 percent of the disparities in fiscal condition across municipalities."[38]

The problems with state aid for property tax relief do not end with their not accomplishing progressive (or any other principled) redistribution. There is evidence that they encourage unnecessary spending. In a summary of the research on the effects of intergovernmental transfers, Ronald Fisher writes, "One important result from much of this empirical work is that lump-sum grants increase subnational government expenditures more than [do] equivalent increases in private personal incomes."[39] Economists have come to call this the "flypaper effect." Money sticks where it hits, and local governments keep and spend some of the money they receive from the state even if the funds are intended to be forwarded to presumably burdened property tax payers.

Another way that large property tax relief schemes can encourage local taxing and spending is illustrated by the following story related to me by a legislative colleague. At the time the state of Minnesota was rebating to homeowners about half of their property taxes (up to a limit of $540). My colleague told of village elders in his rural district, where almost no one was paying as much as $1,080 in property taxes, urging residents to vote for referenda that would raise local taxes. "It sounds ridiculous, but the state will pay half your taxes for you," was their message to their voters.

State aid to local governments suffers, then, from three problems: it is not focused on communities that are in particular need; it creates logrolling opportunities that elevate total state spending; and it encourages local government spending. In the end, whatever efforts the states are making with respect to income inequality are not preventing the inequality within states from growing.[40]

## Conclusion

State governments spend immense amounts of money. The great bulk of that money goes for purposes nearly universally accepted as appropriate, and in those areas improved outcomes are widely deemed important, even crucial. But the clear conclusion of this discussion is that for most of what states do, particularly the activities performed through bureaus, much of that money is spent without sufficient effect. Additional expenditures cannot be expected to yield satisfactory results. When state governments devote resources to redistribution among school districts and cities, they do so haphazardly. In our time, state government is an ineffectual producer of services and a clumsy redistributor of money.

The failure of the budget as the central instrument of state government policy has been established. In the future, in three senses, additional money for state budgets will not be central to improved policy outcomes. First, substantial spending increases are not going to occur. The economy is growing more slowly, and citizens are not supporting big tax increases. Second, much of whatever budget augmentation does occur will go toward keeping expenditures at about their current levels per recipient (per student or per patient). But third, in any event, great amounts of additional spending do not yield commensurate results, given the current ways the states spend money. Even readers who would like to believe that improved outcomes normally flow from increased spending will nevertheless recognize that results of state policy have been inadequate. It has been demonstrated that there is no realistic prospect of producing needed effects by applying large enough amounts of additional money to current organizational arrangements.

Policy must be more than spending money. It must be more than making information available to government employees regarding worthwhile approaches to their work. If the first lesson to be learned from the policy research of the last several decades is that expenditures do not ordinarily produce corresponding results, the second is that knowledge of how to bring about improvements is not necessarily and automatically incorporated into policy. Governments, universities, and foundations have financed research on "what works," taking for granted that what is learned would be put to use. Here and there this information has been picked up and used, but in general that has not happened. In the determination and implementation of policy, starting with elementary and secondary education, research that uncovers more effective ways of carrying out the states' work is not typically applied. Demonstrated improvements are not incorporated into regular practice. To know and to be funded is not to do. We could do better but we do not.

# 4

# Why State Governments Are
# Unacceptably Ineffective

WHEN government goes awry it is usually because people
in positions of power advance their own interests at the
expense of others. Charles Murray contends that "humans acting
privately tend to be resourceful and benign whereas humans acting publicly are resourceful and dangerous."[1] One need not sub-
scribe to his slur on government employees to see that the interests
of public officials, civil servants, lobbying groups, and private citizens can be at odds with those of their fellows.

If people in their public dealings are sometimes as tempted to
watch out for themselves as they often are when engaged in private endeavors, a government not protected against such impulses
will regularly permit some to take advantage of others. Indeed,
before the American Founders put their minds to the question,
prevailing learned opinion had it that a democratic republic likely
could not thrive, saying that it would be done in by self-interest.[2]

The task of this chapter is to account for the inadequate record
in the American states of both policymaking and policy implementation—which largely take place, respectively, in legislatures
and bureaus. The growth and disappointing record of government in the states in this century can be explained in part by the
fact that some of the rationales—the theories—for government
action produced by academics, as well as advice from that quarter on how to structure government, were flawed in that they did

not recognize the need to protect the public from the self-interested behavior of those with governmental power. In this regard much academic theorizing in this century ignored a crucial insight of the American Founders.

## How the Founders Sought to Harness Self-Interest

In James Madison's conception of the American governmental system, the balance and separation of powers play interest groups, both in and out of government, against each other.[3] The Founders were determined to prevent any single "faction" (their word for interest group) or cooperating collection of them from exercising complete control of government, thereby regularly winning un-deserved benefits from the rest of the society.[4] Madison, whose writings were largely congruent with Adam Smith's, saw compe-tition—the institutionalization of countervailing powers—as the foundational device by which a free society protects itself from the self-interested behavior of its members.[5] He wrote:

> Ambition must be made to counter ambition. . . . This policy of supplying, by opposite and rival interests, the defect of better hu-man motives, might be traced through the whole system of human affairs, private as well as public. . . . The constant aim is to divide and arrange the several offices in such a manner as that each may be a check on the other.[6]

In the arrangement that emerged from the Constitutional Con-vention, power was dispersed and played off against power. Each of the states has adopted the same configuration as the national government: a separation of powers into legislative, executive, and judicial branches.[7] The American system was designed, then, so that no one person or governmental organization has the ex-clusive opportunity to decide any serious matter. (This explains why many accomplished businesspeople, eager to translate their success in private enterprise into equally successful political lead-ership, meet with confusion and failure.) Decisions are subject to being challenged, even undone. Those susceptible to being harmed by an action of one branch or level often can induce change in that action by developing allies in a competing entity. Thus is self-interest used to guard against its own untoward effects.

Of course there will be public servants whose concern is not personal and parochial but public-spirited, societal. Indeed, for Madison himself, successful operation of government required that there be leaders as well as ordinary citizens with the latter outlook, a quality which, reflecting an ancient tradition, he termed "virtue."[8] But he and the other Founders believed that to design government under the assumption that persons who work there are mainly motivated by other-mindedness would be to leave the public at the mercy of those in government who are not so predisposed. They wanted to structure government so as to prevent any self-interested individual or group from achieving dominance. At the same time, they expected concern for others and devotion to duty to be nurtured in homes, churches, and neighborhoods. To what extent policy can depend on such concern and devotion from its citizens will be considered at a later point.

The Founders invented a governmental system that harnessed self-interest, albeit incompletely. They intended to expose the branches of government as well as people in the public sector to competition from others. They expected the competition to force accommodations, naturally eroding the benefits that go to self-aggrandizing persons in a monopoly position. Thus they partially protected policy*making* from the ill effects of self-interest, but neither they nor others since have designed a similarly defended system for policy *implementation*. The Founders did not envisage the huge monopoly bureaus of the modern executive branch and within them did not "divide and arrange the several offices in such a manner as that each may be a check on the other." Contemporary American government, national and state, lacks adequate institutionalized protection for society from the self-interested behavior of the people who affect, make, and carry out public policy. We need better governmental institutions for harnessing self-interest to the public interest. Government is inefficient and uninnovative not so much because it is corrupted by wicked people but because we let ordinary people watch out for themselves, sometimes harming others in the process.

Over the years insufficient attention has been given to this central problem of governance. It is the main source of state government's failings and the stuff of the academic discipline of political science. Yet, for a long while it was not a central concern of politicians, nor until recently, of students of the influential disciplines of economics and public administration. The country's resort to distracted legislatures and inefficient bureaucracies has been prompted in part by faulty conceptions of government, defective theories that emerged from academia and for generations provided a rationale for what have turned out to be flawed governmental arrangements.

## How Faulty Theories Have Contributed to Governmental Inefficiency

For a good part of the twentieth century the prevailing theories of public finance and bureaucracy in the United States discounted the importance of self-interested behavior on the part of politicians and civil servants.[9]

The theories of economics and public administration that dominated thought regarding public policy misled for decades in that they conveyed the sense that government policymakers would automatically embody the public interest and that expenditure of funds would equally automatically yield commensurate results. Their influence persists, even in the face of evidence that declared and funded policies consistently fall short of reasonable expectations.

The theory of public finance,[10] a subfield of economics, identified ways that private markets are liable to fail and proposed remedial actions for government to undertake, the idea being that when private markets fail, government should intervene. Market failure thus became an important rationale for government action. However, an implicit assumption of the theory is that "government" is a single, benevolent actor (no separation of powers here!), who is naturally inclined to right the market's imperfections and therefore take the actions suggested by the theory.

Meanwhile, the influential writings of Woodrow Wilson and Max Weber contributed to a widespread conception (with which those authors would not have entirely agreed) of the bureaucrat as somewhat dull, but basically disciplined and likewise inclined to do good, or at least to carry out instructions. Public administration scholars came to see civil servants as neutrally competent and loyally dedicated to doing what they are told. Thus two of the academic disciplines most concerned with government delivered a message that private markets fail, government policymakers stand ready to right those wrongs, and civil servants dutifully carry out the ameliorative actions.

During the great expansion of government in America, the half-century from the election of Franklin Delano Roosevelt to the election of Ronald Reagan, state government spending grew ninetyfold, from $2.8 billion to $258 billion.[11] Let us see how the fields of economics and public administration provided assurance that this money would be well spent.

## *Market Failure as a Rationale for Government Action*

The main intellectual achievement of the professional study of economics is the demonstration that, under certain circumstances, private markets are efficient.[12] For some, the term *efficiency* connotes mechanical pettiness, allowing the significance of the finding to be easily underestimated. But efficiency is no inconsequential technicality.

Competition disciplines; it induces efficiency. In a perfectly competitive economy, government cannot, by takeover, subsidy, or regulation, increase the amount of any good or service demanded and enjoyed by citizens without having thereby to accept a decrease in the available amount of something else (so as to release the inputs necessary to produce more of the first item). That is what efficiency means. The strong presumption emerges that government involvement in a *competitive* economy is unproductive. If government adjusts a previously competitive market, its actions are apt to result in there being fewer goods and services available for the enjoyment of its citizens.[13] The hitch, of course, is that markets fail. Often they are not perfectly competitive; when they are not, competition's disciplining and orienting effect can be lost or weakened. There has long been support for government intervention to correct for lapses in competition.[14]

Market failure comes about in the absence of efficiency-inducing external or internal discipline. If external discipline (competition from other firms) is wanting, a company can charge a price higher than its cost and reap a persistent but unearned profit. As far as internal discipline is concerned, if oversight, motivation, or incentive arrangements are not such as to encourage workers to put out their best efforts, inefficiency occurs. A third form of failure occurs when markets yield an inequitable distribution of income or wealth. The market is blind to whether justice is embodied in the distribution of its riches, so distributional unfairness can be thought of as a form of market failure. These three types of market failure, are quite real, even to the point of being ubiquitous. Market failure is a way that self-interest, when not constrained, causes social harm.[15]

In the early years of this century A.C. Pigou showed that government can institute a variety of payments and taxes to counteract the untoward effects of flawed markets.[16] In doing so he invented what became, for a half-century, the dominant theory of public finance. State government's regulations, appropriations, charges, taxes, and services are sometimes responses to market failure, to self-interest becoming social wrong, and can be understood as applications of Pigou's point. However, public finance economists often left it at that, implicitly assuming that government, having recognized these systematic imperfections of private dealings, would apply a correcting response. What is not confronted in this construction, however, is whether policymakers do, in fact, consistently seek the public good or right the market's wrongs. With little appreciation for the irony, public finance economists, seeing a defective private world that operates badly because of people's unchecked self-interest, implicitly expected government officials (presumably the same kind of human beings) to step forward altruistically and clean up the market's mess.

In the 1970s and 1980s a more sophisticated "positive theory of public interest regulation" developed, leading to a conclusion that government is, in effect, an efficiency-inducing political marketplace.[17] The contention is that waste constitutes opportunity. When the inefficiency of market failure occurs, it can be in someone's interest to correct the inefficiency if they can reap a benefit from doing so. This is a straightforward application to government of the observation that in a competitive private sector opportunities for profit tend to be seized by firms. For example, a potential competitor might lobby Congress to end a company's monopoly position. Government antitrust action could be beneficial to the prospective competitor and to the society at large. The positive theory of public interest regulation attributes to government decisionmakers a tendency, induced by the lobbying efforts of potential beneficiaries, to move systematically to correct market failures. However, as we shall see, sometimes in government as in private enterprises, any of several types of organizational failure can frustrate the efficiency-encouraging effects of competition. Of course, a test of the positive theory of public interest regulation lies in actual government policies. While individual instances of efficiency-inducing lobbying of government occur, nevertheless great inefficiencies persist. For society, net benefits from eliminating inefficiencies would be considerable. However, the costs of identifying sources of inefficiencies and of organizing lobbying efforts to end them evidently exceed the gains for each of the individuals contemplating an effort to change government policy, so large distortions endure. The persistent practice of increasing the budgets of bureaus in the face of little improvement in results is prima facie evidence against the positive theory of public interest regulation.[18] The American political system does not automatically whittle away all major inefficiencies.

Neither traditional public finance theory nor the positive theory of public interest regulation accounts for the inefficiencies in government. Indeed, by ignoring ways in which government fails, both have shored up acceptance of current inefficient public policies.

### The Theory of the Neutrally Competent Bureaucrat

When states and other modern governments act, whether to undo market failure or for any other reason, bureaucracy is the characteristic organizational arrangement by means of which policy is implemented. Half or more of all state spending is bestowed on bureaus. For every person employed by a state legislature, where policy is made, 180 work in the executive branch agencies of the states, cities, and counties that carry it out. The aggregrate totals are 30,000 people compared with 5½ million.[19] Almost all executive branch people are employed in bureaus. This country's most massive bureaucracy is composed of 2.5 million teachers working in public elementary and secondary education.[20]

For decades following the turn of the century, organization theory was dominated by Woodrow Wilson's distinction between politics and administration and Max Weber's image of bureaucracy.[21] For Weber, a bureau was an organization in which people operate within their roles: they are selected, evaluated, and salaried impartially and impersonally on the basis of competence in a given role. In his view, this made possible what could not be accomplished by other forms of organization—fair and capable administration of the large organizations that were coming to characterize government. Wilsonian bureaucrats, fitted by competence to their positions, were disengaged from politics. They accepted and carried out tasks not merely obediently, indeed unquestioningly, but also adeptly.[22] Bureaucracy's "purely technical superiority over any other form of organization" is such, Weber wrote, that "the fully developed bureaucratic mechanism compares with other organizations exactly as does the machine with the non-mechanical modes of production."[23] Thus developed the notion of *neutral competence*, a term of both description and prescription applied for decades by students of public administration to the people who implement government's policies. Politicians make policy, and bureaucrats devotedly carry it out, if not eagerly, then at least automatically. Commenting on the Weberian understanding of organizations, the sociologist James Coleman wrote, "The fact that the persons who are employed to fill the positions in the organization are purposive actors as well is overlooked."[24] Weberian theory diverted attention from the possible interest conflicts between bureaucrats and those for whom they work, and therefore from how bureaucracies operate.

Thus, for much of the twentieth century, influential academic theories in America had it that government consists of legislatures that correct market failures and executive branch bureaus that assiduously carry out the legislatures' policies. These theories encouraged the notions that society's problems would be taken up by policymakers, new ideas for improving government would be picked off the shelf and put to use, and appropriated funds would translate into results. If problems still resisted solution, the indicated policy was to apply more funds or do more research on "what works."

I became aware of this only sometime after I had been responsible, in the then Department of Health, Education and Welfare, for designing and overseeing the federal government's research on and evaluation of educational effectiveness. Year after year, and for a time under my direction, the federal government has sponsored research that has identified numerous effective teaching techniques, curricula, and qualities of successful teachers. One of my accomplishments was to see through to enactment a proposal for a nationwide system of experimental schools. (The project had been the brainchild of Alice Rivlin, my predecessor in the HEW position.) Little that was learned from the experimental schools was replicated elsewhere. In general, actual practice in the vast majority of the country's schools did not and does not reflect much that is known about effective schooling. Applying money and making effective practices available do not automatically yield corresponding results. We do not necessarily do what we know, though influential theories for years lulled us into assuming that we do.[25]

There is a curious asymmetry here: the need for government action arises because the self-interested behavior of private citizens, imperfectly constrained by faulty markets, yields inefficiency and inequity. But for a long while, in much of the academic world, the possibility that government actors also could be devoted to something other than the public interest was not systematically considered as a similar source of societal disorder. It is as though the latter possibility had been dealt with for the ages by the Founders. It had not been. Both the legislative and executive branches are regularly subject to faults at least as serious as those in private markets.

## A New Understanding of Government Failure in the States

We begin to see how things go amiss in state government. A blind spot of many theoreticians and practitioners of public finance and bureaucracy, which persisted throughout most of this century, amounted to lack of recognition that the checks and balances and separation of powers of American government often break down in our legislatures and extend only haphazardly to the internal workings of the executive branch.

Slowly, from the 1930s to the present, academics have developed a new understanding of the malfunctioning of organizations in general and government in particular, thereby formulating a new economics of organization. The recent collapse of the formerly communist regimes has focused attention in the West on the fact that governments in central and eastern Europe had failed to provide desired goods and services. This is prodding Americans to take note of similar inefficiency and resistance to innovation in their own governments' bureaus. In the United States today, as was the case in communist Poland and Russia, government agencies are not subject to the goad of competition, and the absence of opportunity for personal gain in return for outstanding work dampens motivation. It is all but universal practice in the United States not to grant bureau employees a share of whatever "profit" government might gain from efficiency or innovation. A generation ago, it is instructive to note, the economist Jacob Schmookler, after reviewing major innovations in a number of fields, concluded that those innovations occurred only where there was a possibility of profit.[26] Perhaps Schmookler overstated his conclusion. One can point to the origins of computers in the U.S. government during World War II or to research in the facilities of the National Institutes of Health. Still, the reader must determine whether government is to be judged by its exceptions, its outliers, or by its normal activities.

The new economics of organization consists of a not yet consolidated collection of theories in the social sciences that have five features in common: First, the behavior of an organization, governmental or otherwise, is understood as the aggregated actions of the individuals within it. Second, each of those individuals is expected ordinarily to further his or her own interests. Third, the interests of individuals are expected commonly to be divergent from each other and from the purported purposes of organizations of which they are members. Fourth, it is thought to be frequently difficult, as well as expensive, to detect when individuals advance their interests at the expense of others and thus hard to hold them responsible for such actions. Therefore and last, organizational failure comes to be construed as the aggregated actions of individuals behaving in ways detrimental to others because they are not systematically constrained from doing so.[27] (At this level of abstraction one detects elements of these new theories in the Federalist Papers. They can indeed be thought of as a rebirth of Madisonian thinking, though Madison saw more virtue blended with the self-interest in human motivation than do many of his latter-day followers.)[28] The theories from which this understanding is emerging differ in many respects, but what they hold in common promises to revolutionize our understanding of government as well as our ability to bring about improvements.

If politicians and bureaucrats—I have been both—are able to devote their efforts not to public purposes but to hanging on to office or to getting a bigger budget for their agency, some will. The following chapters focus on ways to bring about a convergence of public and private purposes. First, it is important to see under what circumstances those purposes diverge, leaving both private and public organizations subject to faulty performance. While the inefficiency of bureaus and their lack of innovativeness will be examined at length, before doing so we will look at legislatures through the lens of the new economics of organization. This yields quite a different picture from the attribution of automatic public-spiritedness implied by public finance theory and even from the efficiency-inducing tendency hoped for by those espousing the positive theory of public interest regulation. The new academic understanding corroborates the common and disquieting suspicion that people in government are not always about the public's business.

## How Legislatures Operate

Today we face lapses both in setting policy and in carrying it out. It is the executive branch, more than the legislative, that has grown over the years, and that is in urgent need of a correcting design. Still, a sharp distinction between the failings of the two branches cannot be made, because the legislature produces not only the policies carried out by the executive but also the organizations and structures through which the executive does its implementing.

Many legislators believe they have a responsibility to be parochial. Politicians are tempted to find self-protection in dividing their time between railing in the abstract about the wastefulness of government spending and devising ways of grabbing some of the money for the home folks. "You vote your district," legislators say. Voting one's district means taking care of one's constituents, often by bringing home state government construction projects and subsidies for local governments and private firms. A former colleague of mine in the Minnesota House of Representatives seemed bewildered when he heard the suggestion that his first responsibility as a legislator might not be to look out for his district but rather to be concerned for the good of the whole state. "Nobody who thinks like that could ever get elected from my district," he maintained. Similarly, a committee chairman in the Minnesota Senate devised a strategy to minimize opposition to him among interest groups. The senator refused to speak with agents of any groups concerned with issues coming before his committee until they themselves had worked out agreements as to what position the senator should take, his thought being that he could then champion their compromises, ingratiating himself with all without having to take a position in opposition to any. The possibility of his taking a position different from that of any of the groups, or of his having a responsibility for unknowledgeable or unorganized persons or for anyone not in a position to advance his career, appeared not to enter his calculations.

Half of state government spending consists of income transfers to individuals and local governments, not to mention the pork embodied in state offices, hospitals, and parks, which have to be located somewhere. When contemporary students of government construe lawmakers who distribute this money as motivated by a desire to be reelected, their assumption, though simplistic, is less naive than to posit consistently noble motives.[29] Legislators are quick to realize that on election day constituents who are grateful for favors received are more apt to express positive sentiments on a ballot than are those not receiving benefits from the capitol. Thus distributional concerns tend to take precedence in lawmakers' minds over such abstract considerations as whether services are effectively provided, or whether not only one's home district but the whole of the state enjoys economic growth, or even whether justice is on the side of group A rather than group B.

A few years ago it occurred to business owners in the economically depressed resort region of northern Minnesota that their late summer sales might improve if the state's school children were not attending classes at that time. They convinced a legislator to introduce a bill barring the state's entire public elementary and secondary education system from operating before Labor Day. This, its proponents said, would create income and jobs as southern Minnesotans traveled to the northern lakes, bought worms, and otherwise spent money. Legislators representing resort areas solidly backed the proposal, and others, noticing no appreciable organized opposition, acquiesced. The legislation passed, notwithstanding scattered protestations that any money spent at the resorts in late August was not creating new money but was merely shifting money from whatever else would have been bought— movie tickets or school clothes— had people stayed in their home towns instead of taking one last summer outing.

Similarly, on any given day in scores of newspapers across the country one can find a story of a local construction project, new firm, or government agency made possible by a tax break or grant from the state capitol. Accompanying the story is a photograph of the recipient of the funds plus a state official, the local legislators, and a bevy of smiling people employed in the enterprise. To be sure that the point will not be lost on local newspaper readers, the legislators see to it that the story contains an estimate of the number of jobs and the amount of income "created" by the project.

Much of the essence of legislative politics is captured in these anecdotes. Certain lawmakers find ways to please constituents or interest groups without significantly antagonizing anyone. While other lawmakers may or may not be aware of what is going on, they often tend to stifle their misgivings and vote for a proposal in order to maintain amicable personal relations with their colleagues. A simple vote may, in turn, lead to an agreement, usually implicit, of future support for a bill of theirs. (In private conversations with each other, legislators explicitly refer to a proposed racetrack as Representative Smith's economic development project, or a state hospital as Senator Brown's. To support Smith's and Brown's proposals is to bring one's own pet projects closer to being approved.) Whatever reservations skeptical legislators have in these situations often are not nourished by opposing lobbyists or by letters and calls from hostile constituents. Beneficiaries—resorters in the first case, newly employed workers in the second example—are concentrated, organized, and vocal. But those bearing the costs—in the first instance, businesses where people would otherwise have spent their money and that lose sales as a result; in the latter case, citizens throughout the state whose taxes go to pay the subsidy—are generally dispersed and often unaware. Losers far outnumber gainers, but for each losing individual the loss is often likely to be less than the cost in time and money of their participation in an organized effort to stop the project. Spending is redirected, but real growth does not occur for the state as a whole. In the case of the law passed for Minnesota's resorters, since there is no evidence that resort region residents are not themselves now traveling elsewhere in late August—to Minneapolis for a baseball game or Grand Forks for a shopping spree—it is quite possible that spending has not even been significantly redirected to the intended areas.

The troubles do not stop there. For many of the government actions alluded to—recall that each claims to yield economic growth—there is every likelihood that what occurs is not merely a redistribution of jobs and income but actually constitutes a net loss to the state and nation. For a subsidized project, neither the beneficiaries nor the often uninformed persons footing the bill are inclined to calculate whether total statewide benefits of the project exceed total costs. Since the benefiting persons bear only a fraction of the expense (typically, their share of statewide taxes), there is nothing about the arrangement that requires the magnitude of the benefits to equal, much less exceed, the costs.

Usually the folly is not as apparent as in the legislation for the Minnesota resorters, but the motivation for and results of many instances of spending and tax policy are illustrated in the example. A legislative proposal to divert spending from one part of the state to another, or to appropriate tax money, or to borrow funds for new state buildings garners votes because the beneficiaries and their legislators know full well what they stand to gain. Losers are unorganized and often are unaware of what is happening. A legislator is not necessarily inclined to ask whether statewide benefits of new jobs or spending or buildings in one's own district outweigh the costs. It is enough that returns to the constituents at home exceed the locally raised part of state taxes used to pay for the project. Even if the money is not efficiently spent, those potential voters and attentive interest groups on whom it is bestowed are grateful. For them it is income. They may be no more inclined than the legislators themselves to accomplish public purposes with the money. Thus are legislators disposed to concentrate their attention on where money is spent rather than on how productively it is used. One sees clearly why nearly half of state spending (columns D and E of table 2-1) is devoted not even to service provision but to sheer income redistribution, and why this redistribution is not necessarily associated with need or merit. It becomes apparent that much of the money supposedly spent for education, job training, or other service production is better understood as redistribution to influential and grateful recipients— the people *on* whom the money is spent, not those *for* whom it is spent. Heavy lobbying by those recipients—in many state capitols the most powerful interest groups are organizations of teachers and other public employees—reminds politicians of the endorsements, campaign contributions, and volunteer help they stand to lose if their generosity wanes.

The pattern just described applies as much to how legislatures structure bureaus as it does to the diversion of spending from one part of the state to another or to the location of state facilities.

Those potentially benefiting most from a bureau—usually the public employees who will work in it—organize themselves and make known to legislators their wishes concerning its operation. Regulating agencies thus become captives of the regulated.[30] Adversely affected persons, meaning those footing the bill, each of whom has a much smaller stake in the bureau's work, will usually not find it worthwhile to make the effort to organize. Legislators typically put no explicit requirements for producing results on the great bureaucracies of state government.[31] As an example, in Minnesota, lobbyists for public educators had been successful, until as recently as 1997, in making it unlawful for any achievement test to be used statewide that would permit comparison of schools and districts. Madison's vision of subjecting to competition all organizations, public and private, is inoperative in the bureaus of contemporary state government.

A significant share of what happens in legislatures can be summarized in a four-part argument:

—Whether out of a concern for reelection or the conviction that duty obliges such behavior, legislators often seem to perceive part of their role as being a redistributive one, bringing benefits to clearly identified groups on whom they count for support. This behavior is an illustration of the second feature of the contemporary economics of organization (outlined on pages 55–56), in which individuals are expected to further their own interests.

—Legislators see to it that beneficiaries of any single resultant legislative action are made aware of their good fortune, thereby creating potentially grateful contributors and voters. Losers, or those subsidizing the benefits, individually bear such a small fraction of the cost that, though they may be numerous, they are usually passive and are no cause of concern to anyone. Even a legislator who anticipates running for statewide office, recognizing the usefulness of cultivating an appreciative coterie of people as a base from which to make the attempt, might be enticed to participate in the redistribution game. The second and third features of the new economics of organization are thus illustrated, recalling that they attribute divergent interests to individuals and posit that it can be quite difficult to identify instances when persons benefit themselves to the detriment of others.

—From the standpoint of the beneficiaries, who receive much more than they pay for, the ensuing spending and employment constitute improvement; for the state as a whole they are merely redistributive, helping the few at the expense of the many. The legislature has failed, exemplifying the fifth feature of the economics of organization theory, in which people watching out for themselves have received benefits paid for by others because the institution of the legislature is not adequately protected against such actions.

—Since this procedure requires no demonstration that total benefits exceed total costs, it should come as no surprise when, including the expense of administration and the economic distortion caused by arbitrary allocation, some of what legislatures do in the name of service provision and economic development leads to the opposite of growth—unproductiveness, or a net loss in the value of goods and services enjoyed in the state.

"Since the majoritarian process does not force the majority to consider the costs it imposes on the nonconsenting minority, the majority supports wastefully large government as a by-product."[32] The same holds true in this instance: since the redistributive process does not force the beneficiaries to consider the costs they impose on the nonconsenting losers, the beneficiaries—who might well be a small minority of the population—support wasteful government as a by-product.

Much of politics consists of rewarding the appreciative at the expense of the oblivious. Legislators have more on their plates than identifying and correcting market imperfections.[33] James Buchanan darkly summarizes this as follows, "The distributive game that modern democratic politics represents forces the individual legislator to act contrary to any meaningfully defined 'public interest'. . . . The structure of the politics in which they act requires them to act contrary to public interests if they are to survive at all."[34] That flat statement is obviously false, and it is just such generalizations that lead some to write off the good idea underlying Buchanan's hyperbole. Some legislators do seek the public interest. Others accept electoral defeat as the price of standing up for principle. Society's mistake lies in constructing a system on the assumption that altruism is the prevailing sentiment in public affairs. Far better, rather, to honestly recognize our tendencies to self-interested behavior and to look for ways to channel it to social benefit.

Elaborating on the implications of this argument for the structure of legislatures themselves will require another book. Unproductive logrolling cannot be eliminated from legislatures, but it can be inhibited by changes in legislative organization and voting rules. When elected to the British House of Commons, Edmund Burke told his constituents, the electors of Bristol, "You choose a member, indeed, but when you have chosen him, he is not a member of Bristol, but he is a member of Parliament."[35] Burkean behavior by legislators sometimes occurs, but more can certainly be encouraged.

We now turn to the workings of the executive branch, where the unproductiveness of state government is most apparent.

## How Governments and Private Markets Fail in Like Fashion

Both public and private organizations are subject to failure. Indeed, when it comes to producing goods and services, the sources of organizational failure in markets and government are nearly identical. This is the remarkable feature shown in table 4-1. Contemporary research suggests that the flaws of both markets and governments are more pervasive than economists had previously thought.[36] Purely competitive markets are rare, meaning inefficiencies are widespread in private markets. The public sector has many of the same problems as the private, as well as others, so government's own activities are frequently inefficient and government cannot be expected to cure all market failures. Neither sector automatically accomplishes public purposes or prevents some persons from taking advantage of others. The arguments for privatization and socialism are equivalently simple-minded.

Perhaps a more fruitful way of making this point is to note that in both the private and the governmental sector inefficiencies and inequities occur when individual interests are not oriented to

**Table 4-1. How Private and Public Production of Goods and Services Fails**

| Sources of organizational failure | Types of organizational failure | |
| --- | --- | --- |
| | *In private markets* | *In government* |
| *Lack of external orientation to accomplish public purpose* | | |
| Incontestability | Monopoly[a] | Monopoly[a] |
| Good or service not priced | Bureaucratic production[b] Externalities[c] | Bureaucratic production[b] Externalities[c] |
| Distracted monitoring | Organizational slack[d] | Organizational slack[d] |
| *Lack of internal orientation to accomplish the organization's objectives* | | |
| Bounded rationality or imperfect information | Internalities[e] | Internalities[e] |
| *Systematic indifference to the fairness of the distributions of income and wealth* | Income maldistribution[f] | Undue political influence[g] |

a. No competition, so revenue can persistently be higher than necessary to cover costs.

b. Product or service not sold at a price so there can be inadequate pressure from recipients to hold revenue down to costs of production.

c. If no price, tendency to overproduction of negative externalities, underproduction of positive externalities.

d. If monitoring is haphazard, firm or agency can operate inefficiently.

e. Absence of information permits slack: members of a firm or agency can seek their own objectives and slight those of the firm or the polity; innovation is not fostered; costs can be greater than necessary.

f. Market value of a resource or skill tends to determine its owner's income from the market.

g. Political influence of an individual or interest group tends to determine its allocation from government.

public purposes. Exhorting government employees to work in the public interest will be effective on occasion, just as similar pleas made to workers in private firms may sometimes yield desired results. But exhortation's effects are likely to be fleeting in the absence of systematic alignment of private and public interests. Both governmental and private institutions become inefficient or unfair when individuals are not inhibited from benefiting themselves at the expense of others.

Earlier I categorized the efficiency-inducing disciplines imposed on private organizations as being external or internal to the enterprise. That distinction can also be usefully applied to governmental organizations. The left column of table 4-1 lists the three sources of organizational failure: lack of external orientation to accomplish public purposes, lack of internal orientation to accomplish the organization's objectives, and indifference to distributional fairness in terms of income and wealth. Salutary external orientation is present when influences outside an organization persistently constrain the organization from undertaking actions favorable to its members but detrimental to others in society. Correspondingly, an organization might or might not have internal characteristics that press its members to act in ways consistent with the organization's purposes. The other two columns show respectively the ways that private markets and government fall prey to those failures.

### Absence of Efficacious External Orientation

Systematic salutary orientation from outside an organization is wanting when it has a monopoly, or when the good or service it produces lacks a price, or when putative monitors are unable or disinclined to oversee the organization's activities.

MONOPOLY. Monopoly occurs when a public or private entity has an exclusive franchise or an individual or organization has sole access to a resource (for example, because of a patent or a unique location) that gives the monopolist an advantage over potential competitors, or high fixed costs inhibit others from undertaking production (as it would be costly for those potential competitors to reverse that decision and quit production), or increasing returns to scale make entry into the monopoly's market unprofitable for small would-be competitors. Since the entity with the incontestable advantage is not exposed to the rigors of competition, the society is subject to institutional failure; the absence of systematic external pressure on a public or private monopoly leaves it in a position to receive payment in excess of costs.[37]

We are more accustomed to recognizing private sector monopolies than public. Yet government commonly operates by setting up, funding, and issuing mandates to monopoly organizations, its own bureaus. State highway departments have a near-monopoly on road construction. In most of the United States the only school in town available at zero price is operated by the public school board, the sole governmental entity authorized to operate schools. (Friends, reacting negatively to that point, remind me that many people in America do shop for schools. The rejoinder, of course, is that those without means, or who are shut out by bigotry from certain neighborhoods, face a monopoly. It is no wonder that America's educational crisis lies predominantly in the central cities, where racial minorities and other poor people are concentrated. Even those who can afford to move their place of residence in order to find an acceptable school often must bear a considerable price to do so.) Other public services are also organized as monopolies. Ask yourself whether the quality of work provided by the agency from which you get your driver's license or neighborhood street repair is affected by its monopoly status.

UNPRICED GOODS AND SERVICES. The second circumstance shown in table 4-1 in which efficacious external orientation is lacking is when a good or service is not priced. In the absence of a price, that is, if people do not have to pay for benefits they receive or for costs inflicted on others, a good or service is likely to be produced in inefficient quantities and its costs and benefits to be unfairly distributed. The two common manifestations of the problem of unpriced goods and services are bureaucratic production and externalities.

A bureau is an organization producing a good or service, the costs of which are covered, not by sales to willing customers at a price but by a lump-sum subsidy, usually from a single sponsor, and whose members cannot legitimately keep a surplus of revenues over expenses. If the sponsor (a legislature or city council or school board, for example) is not fully knowledgeable concerning what it costs to produce the service, or if the sponsor is not inclined to induce efficiency in the bureau, or if the sponsor is itself the bureau ( a school board), the bureau could easily spend wastefully more than it should. Perhaps even more important, it is most likely not prodded to be innovative and to seek break-throughs that could accomplish increases in output relative to input.

Bureaus are not limited to the public sector. A unit within a private organization, for example a budget or personnel office, might provide unpriced services or goods to other units within the same organization. If those services or goods are difficult to measure, or the processes by which they are produced are not clearly known outside the unit itself, then the unit probably re-ceives little external discipline to innovate or to operate efficiently.

One contemporary strain of research on bureaus begins with the assumption that bureaucrats attempt to maximize their bud-gets. The founder of this strain, William A. Niskanen, recognizes that this assumption may be simplistic, but suggests it may be no more so than the assumption that companies maximize profits or consumers maximize the satisfaction they receive from their pur-chases.[38] An ambitious survey of research on this question con-cludes that evidence is mixed concerning whether bureaucrats are able to accomplish their goal, but "it does make sense to as-sume that bureaucrats attempt to maximize their budgets and to make that assumption the central proposition of a theory of bureaucratic behavior. . . . Indeed, we have not come across any other proposition that would seem to apply as widely to the whole bureaucracy."[39]

Externalities represent another kind of unpriced good or ser-vice. A negative externality is an adverse side effect of production for which the producer does not have to pay, since no market exists.[40] Consider the classic example: pollution. Obviously, a pol-luter, not having to pay a price for the cost the pollution imposes on others, has no inducement to produce less of it.

As with monopolies, externalities in the private sector are more familiar to Americans than are those of the public sector. But since workers in bureaus, government's standard organizational ar-rangement for producing goods and services, may be unmindful of the side effects of their operations, or knowledgeable but not liable, public production can be rife with externalities. For example, public utilities, when subject to rate-of-return regulation by state government, have sometimes resorted to using more capital, and correspondingly less labor, in order to increase the amount of profit allowed. The concomitant unemployment is an externality that comes about because those making the policy, the regulators, are not liable for it. They do not bear the cost. The time lost when clients of a state agency stand in line waiting is an externality; often no one in the agency is accountable for that cost. Externalities occur when people are not held responsible for their work. The most sensational cases of externalities resulting from government operations have come to light in recent years in central Europe, where the worst industrial pollution in the world has been caused, not by private firms, but by government entities. Communist governments let large production facilities there discard waste without regard to the costs they were inflicting on the rest of society.

DISTRACTED MONITORING. Monitoring can be distracted if the putative monitor lacks motivation or information. This problem is more serious in bureaus, but other organizations can also lack assiduous monitoring.

Regular oversight from a legislature could constitute external discipline on a bureau or other organization to accomplish public purposes. Researchers have shown that if a government organization is subject to systematic oversight from a legislative committee, it is capable of efficiency.[41] Such regular scrutiny is uncommon, however, not only because legislators' eyes glaze over at the prospect of being auditors, but also because legislators seldom agree on what they expect from the organizations they create. Minnesota's Legislative Audit Commission, composed of the representatives and senators responsible for overseeing the implementation of state policy, has an excellent staff, perhaps that state government's most competent. But, being small, the staff is able to evaluate any given state program only infrequently. When it does, it oftentimes has difficulty getting the attention of the legislators to whom it reports.[42] I experienced this firsthand when I chaired the commission, finding that my fellow members and I gave less of our time and attention to it than to our many other legislative activities. We were, after all, the same people who had devised the programs that our staff was now scrutinizing. Legislators not on the Audit Commission may be unconvinced that oversight makes sense. One legislator, upon hearing that the audit staff had written a critical report on a program he favored, had this to say to his colleagues: "What the ---- are they doing? They work for us, right? Then why the ---- are we letting them trash our program?" The research finding that legislative oversight can be effective should not lead anyone to expect that it is common practice.

Examples abound of bureaus directing funds to the purposes of their members rather than to the putative beneficiaries of government spending. My colleague Ted Kolderie noted an instance of this in the Minneapolis school district.[43] The district receives supplementary state funds for the education of children from low-income families. Nevertheless, Kolderie found in the city's junior high schools a perfect, but inverse, relationship between the number of low-income children and the amount spent per student. It turns out that senior teachers, who are paid the most, choose to teach in the more comfortable neighborhoods, as the central administration of the Minneapolis district lets them decide at which school they would prefer to work. The supplementary state funds were also consolidated into the district's overall budget, but then, of course, were paid disproportionately to senior teachers. This combination led to a distribution of spending away from low-income students. That is an especially apt illustration of a central point of this book. People, if given the opportunity to do so, will sometimes satisfy their own objectives even if public purposes are frustrated along the way. These teachers were not necessarily selfish or corrupt. They perceived an opportunity to advance their own interests and they did so.

Another, more crass example occurred one year while I was a member of the Minnesota Senate. When one of the teachers' unions issued its legislative agenda, amused legislators noticed in it no reference whatsoever to the education of children. The agenda contained nothing but demands for salary increases and pension benefits. When this was pointed out, the union withdrew the document and reissued it with emendations claiming that the desired increase in remuneration was actually for the children's benefit. Monitoring cannot consistently prevent such practices, any more than it can orient people to direct their activities to public purposes.

The problem of external monitoring is not limited to the public sector. There is a growing belief among economists that some firms, in apparently competitive private markets, might be only haphazardly constrained by competition. If, as is often the case, incomplete information is available about their activities, employees are able to devote efforts and resources to their own interests rather than to those of the firm. Compensation schemes cannot perfectly align private and organizational interests. Still, absence of competition is a greater problem in government than in the private sector. Since "ownership" of public agencies is widely dispersed and citizens cannot sell their "shares," they tend to be less attentive to the efficiency of operation of those agencies than they are to private firms in which they hold stock.[44] In private firms there is also the possibility of bankruptcy. One contemporary school of thought has it that the prospect of being forced out of business by banks, or other lenders, insistent on a level of return at least equal to what is available elsewhere, is the main external discipline on firms and constitutes the principal difference between private firms and government bureaus.[45] Competition for investment funds imposes discipline even on firms with a monopoly in the market in which they sell their products.

As modes of discipline, competition and monitoring have different effects. At its best, monitoring can determine whether those being evaluated are using current technologies as productively as possible, yet it provides no encouragement for innovation or creativity.

Both governmental and private organizations can lack external discipline that would impel them to operate more efficiently and fairly. Monopoly status, bureaucratic organization, externalities, and casual monitoring—table 4-1 shows these four instances of the absence of external orientation to act efficiently and fairly. The great bulk of state spending is susceptible to these systematic failings. The inadequacy of the public schools can be understood by means of the contemporary theory of organizations as resulting in large measure from the schools' being monopoly bureaus. Recall that more than half of all state expenditure is devoted to the operation of bureaus, most of which are monopolies and all of which are subject to the generation of harmful externalities, as well as to distracted monitoring.

### *Absence of Efficacious Internal Orientation*

Economists have traditionally assumed that if an organization is disciplined by external competition, then internal discipline automatically follows. Even where there was not competition, the internal workings of an organization were ignored on the presumption that a firm's owner would maximize profits and in so doing would see to it that every element of the firm operated as efficiently as possible.

Sometimes economists have attributed the same efficiency to bureaus, estimating their "production functions" (the relationship between input and output), as though taking for granted that they are machine-like relationships, humming along smoothly. Lately anomalies have been found: instances of apparently identical organizations, some having much higher costs of production than others. Harvey Leibenstein gave the name *X-inefficiencies* to these incongruities.[46] Charles Wolf calls them *internalities*: instances where individuals in a firm or bureau, because of the difficulty of their being observed or the indifference of their superiors, are able to operate inefficiently or to take benefits for themselves at the expense of their organization.[47]

This situation arises where an individual's interests do not coincide with the responsibilities of the organization in which the individual works, and superiors are unconcerned or lack sufficient knowledge of how employees take advantage of the organization. Lack of internal orientation constitutes an important kind of organizational failure. Since larger numbers of persons in government bureaus than in private firms are not, as a matter of course, held responsible for their work, internalities can be expected to be a greater problem in the government sector as currently constituted than in the private sector.

Whole new subdisciplines are arising in which the problem of internalities is construed as coming about because of absence of information.[48] Two types of information lacunae can be identified: bounded rationality and information asymmetries. If persons are "intendedly rational but only limitedly so,"[49] arrangements and organizations requiring a prodigious amount of contracting and monitoring cannot be expected to operate well. Oliver Williamson argues that because bounded rationality is the ordinary state of affairs, transactions can generally be expected to be incomplete at the time of contracting.[50] Hence people resort to heuristics and rules of thumb, which, though perhaps inefficient, simplify a baffling world. The efficiency envisaged by the neoclassical economics of firms in perfect competition may not even be theoretically possible since superhuman perception and calculation are required. Joseph Stiglitz goes so far as to say that neoclassical economics cannot accommodate information lacunae, that doing so is bringing into being a new "information paradigm."[51] If there is less than full information in economic and governmental life, firms, as well as bureaus, can be expected to operate inefficiently. Potentially profitable opportunities are not exploited, and workers and other agents produce less than would be possible if monitoring yielded better knowledge of what they are actually doing. Once again, remember, though, the possibility of bankruptcy imposes a discipline on private firms that is almost unknown in government.

Contracting—organizations, public and private, can be thought of as collections of contracts—also ordinarily involves asymmetry in the information possessed by the parties.[52] If their interests conflict, which is surely common, the party possessing greater information may be in a position to gain benefits for itself at the expense of other. Parties to a contract may find it in their interest to expend energies to *appear* falsely to be doing what is expected under the contract. Think of an employee whose work is difficult to monitor and who is able to claim credit for more output than is actually accomplished; or a politician who, operating behind closed doors, gives the impression of agreeing with people on both sides of an issue. Again, ask yourself whether information asymmetry contributes to the difficulty of monitoring the work performed by many government employees, from teachers to inspectors to police to social workers to legislators. If monitoring is haphazard or nonexistent, can acceptable productivity be assumed?

## Conclusion

Organizations fail. They fall short of productive potential, miss possibilities for innovation, unfairly reallocate resources. Interests conflict. Organizations, private as well as governmental, are not automatically exposed to external or internal orientation designed to bring the interests of constituent individuals into congruence with the organizations' purposes. Both private and governmental organizations can be flawed and for many of the same reasons.

However, in contemporary America, government organizations are generally less inclined to encourage innovative and efficient operation than are private firms. They are less exposed to the threat of failure. They are more frequently distinguished by monopoly, bureaucracy, distracted monitoring, and internalities. They are apt to cause costly externalities. It is not that private organizations are inherently more efficient than government, but that Americans have permitted their government to be less exposed to the disciplining component of competition, deemed essential by the Founders.

As it exists currently in the United States, government is prone to failure. Almost all state spending goes to bureaus or is redistributed back to local governments and individuals. Bureaus, because they are often monopolistic, are not guided by the discipline of having to meet their costs by selling their products to willing customers. Furthermore, information regarding their operation is frequently difficult for outsiders to come by, and the legislatures that create and fund bureaus oversee them only casually. The other main form of state spending, income redistribution to individuals and local governments, is not focused on needy recipients. However, its apparent arbitrariness is not random. The distribution results from the asymmetry of information available to recipients and payers, the cost of organizing opposition among the payers, and the tendency of politicians—like everyone else, I remind you—to watch out for themselves on occasion.

Just as firms sometimes are prodded, whether by competition or by the owners' desire for profit, to operate resourcefully, under certain conditions a bureau can be enterprising. If bureaucrats are consistently disposed to work toward their organization's objectives; or if they do not receive a fixed wage but rather face large or complex rewards or penalties to shape their actions; or interests do not conflict; or monitoring is easy; or they are directly accountable to the recipients of their services; or legislators exercise consistent oversight; or if a motivating leader impels the organization to act in the public interest—then a bureau can be efficient, perhaps even innovative. Pause a moment to ponder how very rarely those conditions are met. While they exist on occasion, in general they do not *characterize* the bureaucracies of the states in our time.

The great organizations through which the states carry out their work— schools, many hospitals, highway departments and even liquor stores—are monopolistic bureaus. Those working there are not systematically oriented to act so as to accomplish public purposes, but rather toil in the presence of ineffective, dispiriting, and cumbersome rules. Imagine working in an atmosphere where government employees may have private interests at odds with the objectives of their bureau, shirking is often undetectable, innovation is not rewarded, careful evaluation is infrequent, and there is little tradition of paying on the basis of performance. The result: limited incentive to produce desired outcomes.

No one should get by with dismissing this discussion as bureaucrat bashing. The argument presumes that government employees are similar in their proclivities and talents to everyone else. Indeed, one suspects that the widespread demoralization in the civil service is associated with the awareness among its members that perverse institutional arrangements often render their efforts futile. Yet, in my experience many public employees, especially teachers, are personally offended when the suggestion is made that it is imprudent to assume they are regularly public-spirited. Many of them seem fully prepared to attribute consis-

tently base motives to politicians and businesspersons while pro-
testing their own altruism. I have had considerable difficulty per-
suading teachers' groups that the design of government cannot
depend upon an assumption that while others should be expected
to be self-concerned, one class of employee—teachers—consists
of people devoted to the public interest. (Once, early in my time
as a member of the Minnesota House of Representatives, I introduced legislation to facilitate collective bargaining for migrant
workers. In my boyhood, our family's only security lay in my
father's membership in the Brotherhood of Railway Trainmen, so
I well knew the possible value of collective bargaining. To my
surprise I was not able to enlist the support of the Minnesota af-
filiate of the AFL-CIO for the migrant worker legislation. I do not
claim that the leaders of Minnesota's unionized workers at the
time were wicked, merely that they were indifferent to the lot of a
group whom they evidently perceived as not their people.)

The contemporary economics of organization explains the inadequacy of state government. No more than anyone else can individuals in government be presumed to be prone to work
consistently for the common good, though some will do so. Society is left with the inefficiency of bureaucratic production of goods
and services and the unfairness of arbitrary distribution wrought
by legislatures.

Today there is no serious theory or plausible argument that
would lead one to expect state governments, as currently constituted, to meet an acceptable standard. The usual prescriptions of
spending more money and urging better management and hop-
ing for public-spirited behavior are thoroughly wanting. They
emerge from discredited understandings and failed theories of
how government works. Today the urgency of public issues over-
whelms the capacity of government bureaus and the inclinations
of even responsible legislators. Government yields results so deficient that if we do not find better ways to educate our children,
care for the aged, train our work force, and rebuild needed infra-
structure, we face a worrisome future.

# 5

# *Toward State Government That Works: Aligning Private and Public Purposes*

THE FIRST PRINCIPLE of design for effective government services, as suggested by the preceding chapter, must be the alignment of private and public purposes. Continuing to rely on legislative oversight or the spontaneous industry of public employees to improve the current inadequate performance of the states will not suffice. We will now begin working out the ramifications of understanding government restructuring as that alignment. Where government is not carefully structured, it will not work well, it will not be fair or efficient, nor will it be innovative.

## Policymaking as the Design of Government

Unfortunately, many efforts of responsible legislators, civil servants, and public executives are ultimately to no avail. Legislative appropriations and mandates, the exhortations of charismatic politicians, the resolve of able public managers, and the effort of dedicated workers have but short-lived effect if the millions of people who produce public services are not inclined to act in ways that are simultaneously in their own best interest as well as that of the public they are serving. The job of policymaking—whether in state capitals, Washington, D.C., or Moscow—is arranging for such orientation. Bringing about that alignment must come before funding and management, since without it neither money nor administration nor charisma will be consistently efficacious. Many forms of public policy—especially appropriations and mandates—are often ineffective simply because this alignment is not accomplished. Much of policymaking for the provision of services becomes the design of institutions that systematically orient people toward accomplishing societal objectives.

### Inputs Are Not Fundamental

If, as we saw in chapter 3, higher state appropriations do not necessarily yield corresponding results, then we should not expect skilled workers, high-quality equipment, or any other input to produce an organization's or a policy's success. While any of those items might be important, even necessary, none is sufficient unless suitably applied. Without appropriate application, such inputs can, and should, be expected to be wasted, underused, or devoted to extraneous private purposes. Elementary and secondary education is once again illustrative. Not only are expenditures per student today, adjusted for inflation, double what they were twenty-five years ago, triple those of a third of a century ago, and nearly five times the spending of forty years ago, but research has identified numerous effective educational approaches that are not widely used.[1] Not only is money being unproductively spent, but we are also capable of accomplishing much more than we do. These facts are largely explained by our not being oriented to use what we know. Availability of resources, talents, or ideas implies little about how they will be used.

### Incentive Structure Must Precede Management

Much vigorous management goes for naught. When managers, public or private, operate in organizations not characterized by appropriate incentives, their attempts to manage are likely to be frustrated. They can try many things. They can proclaim a mission for their organization, get training for their workers, entreat employees to concentrate on outputs rather than inputs, urge concern for quality, buy up-to-date office equipment, look over each worker's shoulder, commission research on more effective procedures, implore subordinates to be entrepreneurial or to treat clients as though they were customers, call on patriotism, walk around, even stand on their heads.

All of those things are fine, but they are nothing more than management. Management cannot substitute for policy. If workers are not consistently motivated to produce what is expected of the organization—as is sadly the case in most government bureaus—unsatisfactory results will follow. (In the absence of the regular inducement that proper policy provides, will the managers themselves even try the actions mentioned in the previous paragraph?) Some workers will have other interests, and no amount of monitoring, too much of which is demoralizing and costly, will induce the best effort of which they are capable.

Of course bureaus can work well. Some do. Indeed, very occasionally managers introduce incentive systems into bureaus. But that is rare, because typically managers are both constrained from doing so and are not themselves subject to systematic incentives. Here and there in government, idiosyncratic and Herculean management efforts yield impressive effects. Here and there leadership inspires. And of course, sometimes out of sheer public-spiritedness, individual workers will strive to do their best. But all this is likely to be fleeting and weak in the absence of the shoring up provided by the orientation of an enduring motivational structure.

The people of central and eastern Europe recently rose up not only to demand political freedoms, but also because the monopolistic bureaus that produced their goods and services were miserably ineffective. Communist governments tried unsuccessfully to build cars and produce goods in bureaus. No doubt in the Trabant factories of East Germany and in the Soviet food delivery apparatus, some able managers and workers enthusiastically sought to make fine, inexpensive automobiles, and others strove to get fresh vegetables to consumers quickly. But because those clumsy operations lacked effective incentive orientations, management improvements alone would never have made them innovative or efficient. Does anyone believe that an infusion of graduates from the Stanford Business School or the Kennedy School of Government would have had an appreciable effect on the bureaus of the USSR? Similarly, is there any reason to believe that management improvements will make acceptably productive the American public school system, state governments' provision of social services, or any other American bureaucracy not properly arranged to produce the desired results? Skilled leadership and management are, of course, conducive to success, but they are no more sufficient, in and of themselves, than is money. Without suitable organizational orientation, exemplary leadership and management are unlikely even to come forward, and if they do, their effect will not last.

Good management is important but it is not policy: without policy that fosters it, good management cannot be counted on.

## Policymaking Is Design

By now the theses of the previous two sections might seem obvious, but many who are engaged in the study and practice of government cling to the vain hope that the key to improving the public's affairs lies not in social invention, not in systematically aligning private and public purposes, but in changing budget priorities by spending more money or less, training or firing bureaucrats, exhorting workers onward, or simply getting tough. In a free society, if people act self-interestedly, government can be effective only when institutions are organized in such a way that people are motivated to consider not only private, but also social, benefits and costs.

If this felicitous orientation is absent, a policy or management innovation can hardly be called a structural reform. Whatever else they accomplish, government fads such as program budgeting, management by objectives, zero base budgeting, and total quality management do not so change an organization that its members henceforth tend, as a matter of course, to act in ways consonant with the public interest. They ignore the fact that we do not necessarily act upon what we know to work. They depend either on the spontaneous industry of employees or on careful legislative oversight. They do not change the crucial underlying structure of organizations, the motivational structure. Thus they are not structural reforms, and therefore will not have significant, lasting effect.

"Systemic reform," the latest fad among education policymakers, is a case in point.[2] It attempts to articulate national or statewide educational goals, designs curricula reflecting these goals, and follows up with evaluative schemes to determine if the curricula have been successful. Goals 2000 is the Clinton administration's version. The problem with systemic reform is that it is coherence without mechanism. It depends on its proponents to persuade thousands, even millions, of people to accept its approach. Plans and exhortation are not policy.

Policymaking for the provision of services is social invention; it is institutional design. To restructure government is to arrange it so that people acting in their own interest will tend also to accomplish a greater good or, at the very least, do no harm. Where government is not so designed, we should presume that it will not work well. It will not accomplish public purposes. Management and research and funding and mandates have their place, but ordinarily they will not succeed when applied in the kinds of institutional arrangements now characteristic of government in America.

## A Menu for Public Policy Design

It remains to delineate the forms of efficacious arrangement. Only a handful exist.

### Competition

James Madison's vision of a democratic republic ranks in importance with Adam Smith's explication of the economic benefits of markets. In their fundamentals, the two men's insights were identical.[3] Both recognized the tendency, especially when dealing with strangers, for people to act self-interestedly. Both saw the possible ill effects of self-interest, if permitted to run amok. And both were intrigued with the civilizing influence, on free persons, of engagement in political and economic give-and-take. But their central idea was that competition, the institutionalization of countervailing powers, could harness self-interest. If interests were set against interests, largely self-policing systems of politics in the one case and economics in the other could be devised. To this day the possibilities in that idea have not been entirely plumbed.

Somebody ought to order bureaucrats to buckle down, we think. And somebody should figure out what works in good schools, for then surely other schools would pick up those approaches. Somebody should urge public managers to be entrepreneurial. Somebody should come up with a larger appropriation for this or that; then government would do the good deeds that niggardliness is preventing. The blindness inherent in the theories of public finance and of bureaucracy discussed in chapter 4 persists, for no omniscient "somebody" exists, and even if there were such a person there is no way of guaranteeing that he or she would have public-spirited motives. No more can you, I, or the other recipients of appropriations or exhortations be counted on automatically to respond as hoped. If people are frequently self-interested, and pervasive monitoring is neither desirable nor even possible, then setting interest against interest becomes an essential recourse, both to prod and to monitor. The American political and economic systems depend absolutely on competition, an indispensable harness of self-interest.[4]

Flaws in politics and markets are often manifested as excessive costs, which are either wasted or taken as undeserved benefits. Such instances occur when competition is not operating properly, such as when there is a monopoly, or when an organization is not liable for the adverse external effects of the organization's actions, or information asymmetries curb competition's tendency to identify distracted politicians and unproductive employees. Let us call these forms of waste "diversions." These have long been recognized as defects that can inhibit the salubrious effects of competition.

Yet sometimes competition itself can pare down diversions. Recent years have brought a clearer understanding of how this can happen. In the 1950s Kenneth Arrow and Gerard Debreu formalized Adam Smith's idea of competition's invisible hand.[5] They proved that given the conditions of perfect competition (large numbers of buyers and sellers, homogeneous product, no externalities, and perfect information of supply and demand factors), an economy would operate efficiently. Diversions would be eroded because firms not able to curb them would not survive; they would be undersold by others. However, since they assumed everyone in an industry to be making the same product, their attention was distracted from the innovation-inducing quality of markets. In the 1990s evidence has accumulated that some firms in communist countries, especially if their production processes were easy to monitor, had operated fairly efficiently.[6] Lack of innovation turned out to be an even greater economic shortcoming than inefficiency in these economies. Prosperity, and especially increasing prosperity over time, depends more on the introduction of new products and processes than on the efficient use of current technology and resources. Indeed, in the communist years, visitors to central and eastern Europe often observed that much of commercial life, including living standards, resembled conditions in the West a generation or more earlier.

Organizations in competition are prodded to innovate. Sometimes managers and workers do less than their best for the organization. But lagging behind a rival means the possibility of going out of existence, if financing comes from persons or institutions free to transfer their funds elsewhere. Note that this power of competition cannot be accomplished by monitoring. Monitoring at its most effective accomplishes adherence to prevailing norms, efficiency with existing technologies. Competition begets invention.

There are two broad ways of government's using competition for provision of services: direct, where the recipients buy from the producers; and mediated, where government contracts with producers on behalf of recipients. In the case of direct competition, government has four main roles: ensuring that sufficient numbers of buyers and sellers participate for the power of competition to be operative; seeing to it that recipients have sufficient wherewithal to buy the service; adjusting the market (for example, prices) to account for positive and negative externalities; and providing information.

In mediated competition, government employees buy a good or service. For example, government might contract with a firm or not-for-profit organization to purchase computer services, remedial education, or hospitalization. Here government's responsibilities are to specify the task expected of a contractor, to ensure that a number of bidders seek the contract, and to measure results.[7] Because the government intermediaries might lack interest in recipient satisfaction or production efficiency, mediated competition is inherently troublesome. This point is often misunderstood in the academic literature on government contracting. The evident drawbacks of mediated competition lead many to the conclusion that government production is superior. For example, Almarin Phillips notes a number of situations in which mediated markets can produce less than ideal results: when a nonstandardized item is being purchased; when the benefits from the purchase are long term; when information concerning what is being purchased is incomplete, asymmetric, or costly; when there is only a small number of bidders; and when recipients of the service have competing objectives. He favors government production in such situations and sees them as "opportunities to [apply to bureaucrats] incentive mechanisms designed explicitly to overcome such tendencies."[8] John Chamberlin and John Jackson aver that where the standard market failures occur or where distribution considerations are relevant, government production of services is appropriate.[9] Even Joseph Stiglitz, one of the country's most astute critics of markets, slightly misstates the relevant issue. He and his coauthor, David Sappington, note the difference between private firms' being disciplined by investors and government firms' being disciplined by policymakers. But they also implicitly attribute similarity to the two situations, contending that "under public enterprise, the government retains some authority to intervene directly in the delegated production arrangements and implement major policy changes when it is deemed necessary to do so."[10] Well, yes, but all of these commentators implicitly assume that government officials are as motivated to work for the benefit of the service recipients as are the recipients themselves. Of course, the same retort could be made in response to my noting that government has responsibilities even when recipients themselves do the buying.

A promising combination of the two forms of competition applied to education is being tried in an increasing number of states. Charter or contract schools—first made possible by Minnesota legislation in 1991—enable a public education district to contract with the responsible parties in a school to accomplish prescribed outcomes. Under the Minnesota law, the makeup of the school's governing board must be predominantly public school teachers.[11] The school is expected to meet stipulated education objectives but is otherwise quite free to operate as its board sees fit. Meanwhile, under a previous law, school children in Minnesota are free to attend schools in any district. Thus both forms of competition are operative in charter schools. The schools must bid to get a contract from the school district and must be able to attract students, whose families can choose to have them attend elsewhere if they are not satisfied. Note that the logic of this chapter and of charter schools themselves leads to making the boards of school districts responsible for education but not necessarily for owning and operating schools. From that perspective, today's school boards in the United States are subject to a conflict of interest. They own and operate the only entities from which they buy service.[12]

The conditions of perfect competition are almost never met in the real world, so in actual competition some diversions are possible; inefficiency happens. But competition's main power lies in its ability to induce innovation. The fact that consumers, and financiers, can, and will, turn away from a relatively unresponsive or uninnovative organization, public or private, and permit it to go bankrupt and out of existence, constitutes the power of competition. Notice that bureaus funded by legislatures—schools or state hospitals, for example—are rarely nudged in that way. Not only are they not encouraged to innovate, but failure to provide high-quality education or health care as called for by their mission is almost axiomatically seen as indicative of a need for greater funding.

In contemporary debates, competition is sometimes confused with privatization, a much narrower, and largely unhelpful, concept. Because private enterprises are susceptible to many of the same failures as are governmental entities, there is no automatic benefit to be gained from the private sector's undertaking a project previously associated with government.[13] In government, as well as markets, competition is an essential means by which self-interest is civilized.

Contemporary research shows that competition cannot always be counted on to be efficient, because information is oftentimes incomplete. Instances will arise when there are too few producers, when externalities impose unfair burdens, when there are those who cannot afford to participate. Therefore, one must always ask whether there is an alternative. The standard alternative, the monopolistic bureau, comes up deficient because of its inherent vulnerability to the wide range of imperfections already discussed, against which its only defense is the hope of altruism or legislative oversight. Competition remains, as it was for Madison, the foremost institutional arrangement for government's accomplishing, in the public sector as well as the private, the orientation of private interests to broader purposes.

### Adjusting Prices

A second way of aligning public and private purposes is to adjust prices. Government can alter market-determined prices or set them directly in order to overcome the ill effects of monopoly and also to foster efficiency and innovation where, in the absence of government action, goods or services would not be priced at all or would bear prices not reflective of value (and would consequently be produced in too great or too little quantity).

A half-century ago there was considerable enthusiasm for this idea since economists had determined that for any allocation identified as efficient, a set of prices could be calculated that in a free competitive market would yield the desired allocation. Setting those prices, then allowing persons to buy and sell, could potentially be a way for government to accomplish its goals without having to go through all of the work of requiring that each company in the country produce a specified amount of goods and services.[14]

In the end, proposals in communist countries to calculate and set prices at levels that would have resulted from a competitive market were not implemented, perhaps because doing so smacked too much of mimicking a market system (which of course it does). Nevertheless, government authorities in those countries did set a myriad of prices (though not inspired by any desire to simulate a competitive market), only to have the practice founder, not only because of the formidable computations required, but also because the opportunities for mischief were so numerous.[15] As of the late 1980s, the Soviet government was still setting 26 million prices.[16] Such pricing was a major reason for the food supply problems of the early 1990s in the Soviet Union. Politics required that if government were to determine certain prices—of food, for example—they had to be set low. Farmers, however, ultimately declined to produce goods at prices below their cost of production, leading to serious shortages.

Notwithstanding the difficulties associated with large-scale price setting, there remain ways for government to use the price system to foster efficiency and innovation.

By requiring a natural monopoly to set its price near marginal cost, government can reap for society the benefits of economies of scale while preventing the gouging normally associated with monopoly. (Without a subsidy, a firm in this situation cannot operate without a loss if its price is set exactly at marginal cost, because at that point marginal cost is less than average cost and thus total revenue is less than total cost.)

Another type of price setting for achieving societal objectives is the introduction of a price where previously there was not a market. This possibility arises in two situations: when government contracts to purchase a good or service (medical services or printing of documents) at a price from a private or public producer rather than depending on bureaucratic production, and when government encourages or discourages production by creating or adjusting a price. I was alerted to an instance of this practice while driving through Sydney, Australia, with the Speaker of the New South Wales Parliament. He pointed out a building, saying that it housed a private printing firm that, until recently, had been a government bureau. He had discovered that the actual cost of his business cards, when printed by the bureau, had been ninety-nine cents each. Convinced that the cards need cost only pennies apiece, he and others moved to transform the bureau into a private firm with which the Parliament and other government and private bodies now contract for printing services. By stipulating the price it will pay for privately or publicly produced services rather than depending on bureaucratic supply, government can step in efficaciously where previously there was an absence of salutary external or internal orientation.

Similarly, government can influence the amount of an externality that will be produced by setting a price intended to discourage or encourage production or consumption. Here is the most transparent case of aligning private and public interests. Pollution is, in effect, a cost of production, one extracted not from the generator of the pollution but rather from those affected by it. Levying a fee on the polluter that reflects the cost of the pollution on others induces the polluter to take the public interest into consideration. Revenues from the fee can be used to clean up the remaining pollution or otherwise compensate those hurt by it. Private and public interests are aligned. Taxing cigarettes and effluents are other examples of this practice.[17] In cases of goods and services that have positive rather than negative effects on others, such as education, alignment of private and public interest can come about through subsidies.

## The Importance of the New Economics of Organization

The two modes of policy design implied by the new economics of organization, competition and adjusting prices, are hardly unfamiliar. So how important is this new academic wrinkle on Smith and Madison's theme?

At this time, no other theory explains as broad a range of organizational behavior as does the new economics of organization. In light of its critique of government bureaus, no plausible theory would lead one to expect those bureaus, as now organized, to be efficient or innovative. They vainly depend on the efficacy of spending and rules and are largely devoid of appropriate orientation since they rarely embody either competition or allocation by price. Creditable performance of bureaus, as they are now structured, depends on idiosyncratic or heroic efforts.[18] But let us be clear. There is a basic difference between policies of competition and price setting. Government's stipulating prices is a policy of problematic efficacy in the United States, for the same reason that setting prices in Moscow failed. The larger the number of individual allocation or pricing decisions made by government, the larger the number of opportunities for those in government to get or give undeserved benefits, or, said another way, for their self-interest to get in the way of public purposes. Competition is a largely self-policing discipline; when it is operating, the number of decisions needed to be made by government is greatly reduced, thereby correspondingly reducing the number of possible occasions for misallocation.

Still, the new economics of organization leaves us in a predicament: any policy that does not include systematic orientation of involved individuals toward accomplishing the policy's public purposes can be expected to fail. But if everyone, including policymakers, can be expected sometimes to act egoistically at the expense of others, there may be no audience for that prescription. Most of this book, with the exception of the section on legislatures in chapter 4, has proceeded on the assumption that policymakers perceive a public purpose and decide on a policy to bring it about, seeking institutional arrangements that will orient the interests of the individuals involved toward accomplishing the broader objective. However, consistency requires regarding politicians, like others, to be frequently self-concerned and thus not necessarily determined to ascertain the public will and to embody it in effective policy.[19] What about the private interests of the policymakers?

## Who Oversees the Overseers?

The argument of this chapter thus far sees government's inadequate performance as emerging from a lack of alignment of private and public purposes. To this point, the discussion has sometimes begged the question whether the interests of policymakers, the persons designing the implementing structures, might be at odds with those of others in the society.

Since legislators—policymakers—can be as egoistic as the next person, and because they are elected from districts that are each much smaller than the whole of society, many feel it is their responsibility to be parochial. In legislatures, misalignment of private and public purposes is manifested in the granting of benefits to concentrated, organized interests at the expense of others. Legislators tend to look for ways to bestow boons on appreciative interest groups and to pay for them in ways so dispersed as to leave the (tax)payers in the dark. There is nothing about this situation that necessarily inclines anyone to demonstrate that total benefits exceed total costs. Thus are produced inefficient bureaus, regulatory agencies dominated by the interests being regulated, and tax breaks and aid formulas that grant funds not to the needy but to constituents of powerfully placed individual legislators. Legislators do not systematically oversee this situation—they created it—and besides, many of them find oversight tedious, as well as electorally unproductive.

To confront this situation, Professor Susan Rose-Ackerman of Yale University proposes a controversial third category of policy design that I will call *principled oversight*.[20] Rose-Ackerman suggests that courts should strike down laws that, while purporting to be in the public interest, actually grant special favors and at a cost to others greater than the benefit to the favored group. She would have the courts regularly conduct cost-benefit analyses of government programs. Then, in any case where measured societal costs exceed benefits, unless the legislative branch has explicitly declared that to be its intention, a court could invalidate the legislation. The advantage of the Rose-Ackerman proposal is that it structurally reduces the number of opportunities in the society for successful rent, or boon, seeking. (*Rent seeking* is the term used by economists to denote the effort of those trying to get undue benefits from government.) Her proposal works by proscribing a whole class of organizational failure—the instances where societal costs exceed benefits. The proposal satisfies a goal of institutional design: reduce the number of occasions when rent taking can occur.

The Rose-Ackerman proposal shares a weakness with bureaucratic production. Both depend on rules to accomplish desired behavior, though her proposal possesses the advantages that the rule (the cost-benefit criterion) would be followed because of the authority of the courts, and compliance could be fairly straightforwardly monitored by means of the cost-benefit calculus.

However, the Rose-Ackerman proposal is subject to another shortcoming that has to do with how benefit is measured in cost-benefit analysis. In that discipline, the benefit of a project is the aggregated dollar value that persons are willing to pay for the product of the project. The value of a bridge or road or swimming pool is whatever people would pay to use it. Of course, willingness to pay depends on each individual's economic wherewithal and preferences. Presumably some deserving, but destitute, people sorely desire a new bridge or road or pool, but are not prepared to pay for it since they lack money. Their desire would carry no weight in cost-benefit analysis. Thus, if policymakers disapprove of the current distribution of income, they might not accept the benefit calculation of cost-benefit analysis. They might be willing to give up some efficiency in the society for a change in the distribution of income and might put more weight on the preferences of the poor (or of other groups) than does the market. In such a case, they would see no reason to abide by the cost-benefit criterion and would be outraged at the idea that the courts should be empowered to overrule their judgment in this regard. Rose-Ackerman would respond that a legislature's action should be permitted to prevail in such a case, but only if it explicitly stipulated that it understood that its action was at odds with the cost-benefit criterion, yet favored it anyway. But then what is to be gained by her proposal?

The new economics of organization has developed in part as a reaction to the costliness of resorting to the courts for the settlement of disputes. The contention, by adherents to the new discipline, has been that careful designation of property rights with subsequent private negotiations and competition is generally a more efficient, less costly way of dealing with organizational failure than is resolution by either bureaus or courts. In that sense, because the Rose-Ackerman proposal would impose settlements rather than have them worked out by contending parties, it is somewhat at odds with the thrust of the new economics of organization.

The Rose-Ackerman proposal does not entirely resolve the "who oversees the overseer?" question. But then neither did the Founders when they too resorted to a separation of powers, "divid[ing] and arrang[ing] the several offices in such a manner as that each may be a check on the other."[21]

## Conclusion

The policymaking lesson of the contemporary economics of organization is this: construct policy so that individual and group interests coincide. In general, where this coincidence is lacking, policy objectives will not be met. In particular, in the absence of this coincidence, state governments' policy ambitions will be realized only episodically and only after exceptional efforts that defy replication. Usually, achieving coincidence of individual and group interests will mean so shaping incentives that egoistic persons will automatically accomplish public purposes. In a free society, where people are naturally self-interested, only competition between freely contracting individuals and groups can systematically harness that self-interest. The efficacy of appropriations, mandates, skilled management, professional norms, and inspirational leadership should be expected to be weak or fleeting in the absence of competition's systematic alignment of private and public interests. Alternatives to competition depend on a deus ex machina, the assumption that someone, somewhere, will impose non-self-interested policies.

We have reached an impasse. Because self-interestedness is widespread, competition is an essential civilizer. But as life within a society also requires some public-spiritedness, competitive arrangements, as well as others, for meeting public purposes need to be designed. From where will the public-spiritedness come?

# 6

# *Beyond Incentives: Community as Policy*

NOTWITHSTANDING the success of the economic method in explaining much of human behavior, a huge amount of literature dating back thousands of years argues the wrongheadedness of construing society as an aggregation of self-interested individuals. I will not conduct a thorough review of those arguments here. My purpose is more limited: to seek efficacious policies. The relevant criticisms of self-interest theories point to another form of policymaking that along with competition is one of the only two broadly effective, largely self-regulating instruments available to a free people for accomplishing public purposes.

Are persons only self-interested, and if not, can theories resting on an assumption that people sometimes act out of altruism (either love or duty) provide a basis for policy? Criticisms of the argument made in chapters 4 and 5 answer no to the first part of that question and a qualified yes to the second. If those criticisms are persuasive, then competition is not the sole dependable policy method available to a free people.

There is much that twentieth-century self-interest theory cannot explain. It cannot fathom why people vote. (Some effort is involved, and the effect of a single vote is almost always so tiny that a calculation of one's benefits and costs could lead to a decision not to bother.) It cannot provide an understanding, in many circumstances, for why, without special incentives, any member of a large group would produce public goods,[1] since presumably everyone would wait for someone else to do so, then free-ride. Self-interest theory cannot account for why anyone would give anonymous contributions to charity, take back to the owner a wallet found on the street, or leave a tip at a restaurant to which she intends never to return.[2] It does not know what to make of courage in battle or faithful spouses or diligent, unmonitored workers. And, to foreshadow a conclusion of this chapter, self-interest theory is blind to the possibilities for exceptional organizational effectiveness where people are motivated chiefly by love or a sense of responsibility.

Competition is indispensable in politics and markets, where it disciplines strangers. But if it is to have satisfactory results, even competition requires of its participants some sentiments other than self-interest. The general public, and perhaps other academicians, may be unaware that, whatever the case in times past, contemporary economists recognize the existence, even the necessity, of these other qualities.

Douglass North, a recipient of the Nobel Prize in economics, says, "It is hard—maybe impossible—to model . . . a polity with wealth-maximizing actors unconstrained by other considerations. . . .We need to know much more about culturally derived norms of behavior."[3] An earlier Nobel laureate, Kenneth Arrow, wrote, "A close look reveals that a great deal of economic life depends for its viability on a certain limited degree of ethical commitment. Purely selfish behavior of individuals is really incompatible with any kind of settled economic life. There is almost invariably some element of trust and confidence."[4] "We had better recognize from the start," asserted the economist's economist, Joseph Schumpeter, "that exclusive reliance on a purely altruistic sense of duty is as unrealistic as would be a wholesale denial of its possibilities."[5] Jane Mansbridge has assembled a collection of essays by scholars from several social sciences, the common thread of which is "reject[ion of] the increasingly prevalent notion that human behavior is based on self-interest, narrowly conceived."[6]

These comments by twentieth-century academicians are reminiscent of James Madison's view that the governmental arrangements he devised would demand more than self-interest on the part of Americans. At Virginia's convention called to consider ratification of the Constitution, he contended that politicians would not "do every mischief they possibly can." He continued, "I go on this great republican principle, that the people will have virtue and intelligence. . . . To suppose that any form of government will secure liberty or happiness without any virtue in the people, is a chimerical idea."[7]

So far, if you accept the testimony of the persons just cited, we have only recognized that pure selfishness is not sufficient for the successful operation of competitive political systems and markets. Competition requires, in its participants, a modicum of virtue: trust, industry, respect. But we are looking beyond competition. The goal of this chapter is to identify noncompetitive social arrangements, dependent on the more heroic virtues of love or duty and capable of better carrying out some of the functions now performed by government. If competition can sometimes *harness* self-interest to public purposes, are there also circumstances where people can be counted on not to compete with others but to *transcend* self-interest and to work spontaneously for the welfare of others?

## The Communitarian Critique

Communitarianism is the conviction that humans are properly understood not as autonomous and self-interested individuals but as social creatures, whole only in groups and devoted to others in those groups. For our public policy purposes a community is an organization, membership in which ordinarily draws people to seek the benefit of others.[8]

Communitarianism stands against the liberal idea that underlies the economic vision of society and thus underlies the new economics of organization. Here liberalism takes its definition from its Latin root, *liber*—free. Liberalism, drawing from the nineteenth-century meaning of the word, not the colloquial understanding in our time, is the idea that the autonomy, the freedom, of the individual is fundamental to any meaning of social welfare, fundamental even to any conception of what is good in life. The critique of liberalism from contemporary communitarian philosophers, with Alasdair MacIntyre in the lead, is that community is necessary for the good life, but liberalism has given us instead loneliness and anomie.[9] Community is necessary if politics is to yield the public good, but we have gotten government by self-concerned interest groups indifferent to the effects of policy on others.[10] Community is necessary for the generation of virtue but, turned loose to follow our base inclinations, we have become greedy and dissolute.[11] In undermining community, liberalism has brought us to ruin.

Liberals respond that in a free country people can choose community if that is what they truly want. John Rawls, the most influential liberal philosopher of our time, writes in his magnum opus, *A Theory of Justice*, "Although justice as fairness begins by taking the persons in the original position as individuals . . . this is no obstacle to explicating the higher-order moral sentiments that serve to bind a community of persons together."[12] Similarly, Allen E. Buchanan contends that "liberal individual rights provide valuable protections for the flourishing of community."[13]

Communitarians are unpersuaded. If individual autonomy is antecedent to any conception of the good in life, if individuals are at a remove from any interests or attachments they might take up, perhaps they are predisposed never to be immersed in community. Michael Sandel states, "On Rawls's view, a sense of community describes a possible aim of antecedently individuated selves, not an ingredient or constituent of their identity as such. This guarantees its subordinate status."[14] Thomas Nagel goes further. For him, the liberal understanding of the individual offers "not just a neutral theory of the good, but a . . . conception according to which the best that can be wished for someone is the unimpeded pursuit of his own path, provided it does not interfere with the rights of others."[15]

The communitarian thesis has it that in a society dominated by the liberal idea, individuals are so loosely connected that they are unlikely to become intensely altruistic. Perhaps, in order to develop relationships with others strong enough to counter selfishness, a person's very understanding of self must include membership in community. But that is conjecture, not a finding. We need to see whether in fact, in America, there are communities in which devotion to others accomplishes public ends. Are there groups in which members customarily and spontaneously provide services for each other and even perhaps for persons outside the community, services that otherwise might be less successfully rendered by government? That is what we are endeavoring to determine. The communitarian critique of liberal society finds community formation difficult in America today. Still, that does not render communities impossible, but neither does the wish that they exist make them materialize. It is one thing to note instances here and there of altruism, but something else to make a case that such behavior can be counted upon.

## Varieties of Community

Four schools of communitarian thought, of varying usefulness for our purposes, can be identified. We will find among them the instrument we seek, but will also observe that some types of communitarianism are of little use for public policy, despite their considerable importance for other purposes or their attractiveness in a more utopian world.[16]

### Inclusive Community

One contemporary form of communitarianism can be termed inclusive in two senses: it can be construed to contain the other forms, and it rests on the notion that the whole country is, or should be, a community. No American is more responsible for the recent renewed interest in community, so understood, than Amitai Etzioni.[17] The prolific Etzioni has written a number of books on the subject as well as inspiring the formation of several journals of opinion, creating numerous discussion forums, convincing people from coast to coast to sign a communitarian platform, and leading what he calls a communitarian movement. This movement embodies two basic ideas: all citizens have responsibilities to others to foster the common good, and core values in this country should be not only celebrated, but inculcated in, and expected to be held by, everyone. These include respect for others, a devotion to hard work, and commitment to democracy in general and to the Bill of Rights in particular. But Etzioni believes that the proliferation of rights in contemporary America both emerges from, and fosters, a selfish individualism. He proposes a moratorium on the enunciation of rights during which time we remind ourselves of our obligations to others. (For those not yet convinced that the generation of rights has gotten out of hand, he cites people who insist that women have a right to use men's rest rooms whenever they want and others who would attribute to prisoners a right to the use of artificial insemination.)[18]

Etzioni longs for an America that is more fraternal and less nasty, more generous and less selfish, more proud of its founding ideas and less iconoclastic. His communitarianism is moderate, eclectic, secular; his tent is large. Personally, I admire this vision and share the hope that Americans will regularly act in the interests of other citizens, and I expressed my commitment to these ideals by being one of the original signatories of Etzioni's communitarian platform.

Etzioni's policy recommendations fall into two categories : those that strengthen the small communities of which the nation consists, particularly the family; and those that encourage tolerance, respect, and kindness in all. The first of these will be considered below in a discussion of mediating communities. The public policy effectiveness of the second depends on an unlikely mass conversion. Its proponents exhort their fellow citizens to be more other-minded, to think of the nation as one large community, a family. When, in a celebrated speech at the 1984 Democratic national convention, Mario Cuomo pleaded for all to view the United States as a family, he was invoking inclusive communitarianism. No doubt, throughout the country, his evocative metaphor and eloquent delivery led many Americans to wish they were bound together like family members. Walter Mondale saw "my America is a community, a family, where we care for each other." "I see America as a family," Lyndon Johnson had said two decades earlier.[19]

The metaphor is fundamentally flawed. The United States is

not a family. No individual state is a family. In large measure, we need government because our relationships with others in the polity differ from our ties to family members. We normally cherish and accept responsibilities for family members, but only infrequently treat strangers in that fashion, notwithstanding the Biblical injunction concerning how we are to approach our neighbor. Perhaps we aspire to self-improvement that would lead us to love all persons, but how many Mother Teresas are there among us who achieve that state? The alluring vision of inclusive communitarianism implies a policy of exhorting people to act toward all as they do toward family. On rare occasions political leaders succeed in getting us to behave that way. One thinks of Churchill's inspiring oratory during World War II, John Kennedy's Peace Corps, and Martin Luther King's "I Have a Dream" speech, but any such list is very short. Exhortation is the technique of the inclusive communitarian, but as an instrument of public policy it lacks dependability and persistent effect. Indeed, over time, as America's ideological and ethnic diversity increases, perhaps fewer and fewer occasions arise when fellow-feeling brings the whole of the country together to work on anything.

The price of the breadth of inclusive communitarianism—remember, we are all members of its community—is a reduction of what members have in common. But, sad to say, people with whom we have little in common are not able to hold our consistent loyalty and affection. Only episodically do citizens act in the interests of the whole country or their whole state. Inclusive communitarians wish for, but have not found, the moral equivalents of war, causes that fire the fervor of all. (In our cynical and factious time, even war is not the moral equivalent of war.) The demise of the communist regimes of central and eastern Europe has demonstrated the extreme difficulty of inculcating among masses of people persistent sentiments of generosity to strangers. This had been anticipated by Friedrich Hayek in *The Road to Serfdom*, in which he described socialism's flaw as the hope that altruism could inspire consistent cooperation among large groups of people.[20] He saw altruism as being dependably efficacious in small groups, but contended that there is no substitute for competition when dealing with large groups. Referring to the formerly communist countries, a disillusioned Robert Heilbroner discusses the vain socialist longing for "a kind of civic awareness which could provide the necessary incentives, giving us a society driven by higher rather than lower promptings."[21] It did not happen.

Devotees will continue to try to generate, in themselves and others, those higher promptings, but in the broader of its two understandings, inclusive communitarianism provides no consistently strong policy instrument. It is not capable of regularly, predictably, producing social benefits, and its policy instrument, exhortation, carries nowhere near the power and pervasive influence of competition. In the end, inclusive community is not so much a policy as an aspiration or, as Etzioni puts it, an attempt to build a social movement. One wishes it well, but fears that such a movement will be no more successful than previous equally admirable attempts to construct what Herbert Croly, earlier in this century, called a "religion of human brotherhood."[22]

### Republican Community

Robert Booth Fowler has rightly called *republican community* a contested term.[23] For some it evokes an image of America before the drafting of the Constitution, when, for a moment, this country had an opportunity to see and define itself as a collection of pursuers of the common good rather than one of self-seeking individuals.. Thoughtful observers of this period, such as Gordon Wood or Robert Bellah or J. G. A. Pocock, contrast the image of an America of shared aspirations, cooperative governance, and widespread involvement in politics with the country as it is today.[24] They lament the America that emerged from the constitutional era defined by the ideas of individualism, especially the Bill of Rights. America became Lockean, liberal, verging on Hobbesian, with its politics dwelling more on the clashing of interests, rather than on a search for the public interest.[25] It is that search, the devotion to the commonweal, that provides the usual meaning of republican community.

Try to think of this understanding of republican community as a version of inclusive community, for its power, such as it is, rests in viewing a whole state, or all of America, as one cooperative group.

A contemporary echo of republican community can be heard in the current call for a strengthening of civil society.[26] This takes the form of pleas for participation in voluntary associations from labor unions to bowling leagues, on the grounds that governance of a free people depends upon, indeed partly consists of, engagement in these private associations. Note the Tocquevillian point that these associations depend on a prior generation of other-mindedness. "Voluntary associations," writes Peter Berkowitz, "not only generate 'social capital'. . . they *presuppose* it."[27] How that generation takes place is rarely taken up in the current discussion on civil society, though it will be briefly considered later in this chapter.

I offer a different meaning of the term *republican community* from either of the two just discussed. Though perhaps somewhat unconventional, it has the merit of describing the dominant understanding, in my experience, of republican community among the politicians, reporters, lobbyists, and interested citizens who are actually involved in politics. In today's America, the surviving form of republican community accepts liberalism and accepts the struggle between interests as the driving engine of politics. But devotees of the current form of republican community acknowledge that the competitive machine requires restraints. People need the virtues of tolerance, industry, trust, and at least a grain of concern for the welfare of others.

Republican community, understood thusly, differs from inclusive community in its aspirations, in that they are much less ambitious. James Madison was its first adherent. Introducing competition, "supplying opposite and rival interests," into market and government was his "constant aim."[28] He and his latter-day followers, including many contemporary social scientists, have contended that self-interest must be mitigated by "virtue," that competition needs to be civilized by social norms that restrain self-interest.

Republican community, as it has thus come to be understood in America, also differs greatly from the classical conception of virtue, which included the view that a central purpose of government was to form in the character of its people such qualities as justice, loyalty, self-control, and courage. The main subject of Plato's *Republic,* the first great treatise on government, is education. The pervading argument throughout the *Republic* holds that virtue is knowledge; knowledge can be taught; teaching is so important that it must be controlled by the state.[29] A contemporary, and less extreme, version of this idea appears in *Statecraft as Soulcraft,* the title and message of a book by George Will. For him "the purpose of politics is to summon . . . the better angels of our nature."[30] Though Will intellectually outnumbers legions, when he attributes the function of moral formation to government he has few contemporary allies, which is a sign of the ascendancy of the muted American conception of republican virtue.

Those espousing the pale contemporary version of republican community not only have not expected government to be the generator of character, they also have in common a certain disinterest concerning where the restraining virtues are instead to be developed.[31] That was more understandable in Madison's time, when he could take for granted that family and church would mold their members, developing the graciousness, civility, responsibility, and generosity necessary for successful social, economic, and political life.

Again, as with the inclusive communitarians, I share the hopes of the republican communitarians. In this chapter we seek, though, a policy instrument. In its current form, republican communitarianism, for all its attractiveness, indeed its necessity, is not a separate policy instrument, but an adjunct to, a lubricant for, a civilizer of, competitive politics and markets. If the contemporary form of republican community were all there is to community, competition would be the only broadly effective instrument of policy, for one could not depend on altruism.

## Participatory Community

Historian John Patrick Diggins would describe inclusive and republican communitarians, as discussed, as lacking an "ethic of ultimate convictions."[32] The remaining two forms of community to be presented, participatory and mediating, are not, according to some, subject to that same observation. Participatory and mediating communities also differ from inclusive and republican communities in that they are not universal, but more specific. Rather than dealing with the whole of society, they focus on the members of one's own group, as it is in these subgroups that one tends to place intense, even categorical, loyalties.

Participatory community is a contemporary manifestation of a recurring American phenomenon: the countercultural attempt to create small organizations in which individuals can become lost in the group.[33] As was the case in the past, today's participatory communitarians are inventive, romantic, angry, egalitarian. For them community is created by persons dissatisfied with existing social arrangements, large and small, a substitute for traditional forms of family, religion, government, and business.[34] Participation—empowerment—is essential to human dignity, and therefore governmental and other decisionmaking must take place mostly in small milieus where people live and work.[35] All this the commune dwellers in the second half of the twentieth century have in common with the creators of the utopian socialist settlements of nineteenth-century America.[36]

This sweeping description glosses over differences among several strains of participatory community. Robert Booth Fowler identifies three varieties: participatory community as way of life, participatory community as a manifestation of populism, and participatory community as a cautious, "chastened," search for cooperative, efficacious small groups.[37]

PARTICIPATORY COMMUNITY AS A WAY OF LIFE. The 1960s' zeitgeist lives among contemporary participatory communitarians who seek a way of life. They reject traditional, and especially large, organizations of all kinds, pursuing identity and worthwhile labor in small groups and local activities. These activities might be linked or consistent with such national efforts as the antiwar, antisexist, or civil rights movements. Local community organizing to stop construction of a highway, to make a neighborhood safer, to protest arms proliferation, the operation of a nuclear power plant, or the hiring practices of a university is as much a search for, and affirmation of, a personal identity as it is a political statement. The

New Left had it that small, local "participatory democracies" would be a cure for the alienation resulting from domination of the society by large organizations of various kinds.[38] Kirkpatrick Sale designs and proposes communities containing a few hundred or a few thousand people in his book, *Human Scale*.[39] He hopes that in towns of that size, ordinary life, including business and politics, could consist largely of close, even intimate, relationships among people who know each other well and look out for one another.

Associations of people brought together by a desire for racial or gender solidarity can also be thought of as instances of participatory community. Indeed, the term *community* is most used today by those referring to such groups—"the African-American community," "the Latino community," "the Gay and Lesbian community."[40]

PARTICIPATORY COMMUNITY AS POPULISM. A contemporary form of populism—not the sweeping protest movements of the last turn of the century, but small, local, problem-solving efforts—might be called participatory community. Harry Boyte is a theoretician and a leading proponent of this type of participatory community.[41]

Boyte sees politics as having become distant from people. In this century, local politics has been depreciated as policymaking has become increasingly national. Political work has come to be performed not by engaged citizens, but by elected delegates. Citizens are not participants, but spectators. Boyte identifies "free spaces . . . public places . . . which people 'own,' in which groups of people are able to learn a new self-respect, a deeper and more assertive group identity." Citizens come together out of recognition of some common goal—to build a playground, start a store, make a neighborhood safe. This continues old American "traditions of mutual aid, town-meeting government, and religious covenant." In his view, all of this depends, though, on these groups' *doing* something. Boyte is hard-boiled. His citizens are self-interested (though he takes pains to assert that self-interestedness need not be mere selfishness).[42] They might have a common goal or maybe only a common problem. Confronting this commonality generates cooperative work and, perhaps, a deepened sense of citizenship and responsibility for the larger republic. Boyte dismisses much current talk of community, which he sees as sentimental and impractical. He views communitarians, such as Etzioni, as merely espousing values or seeking mutual understanding, which Boyte believes is much less promising than tackling problems. Boyte believes that engagement in socially productive work "neither presupposes nor anticipates normative consensus or 'bonding'"; rather, "respect and awareness of commonality among diverse groups are more frequently the products of pragmatic work."[43]

Boyte does not claim to be a communitarian. In its emphasis on individual pride, assertiveness, and autonomy, his work depends more on the liberal vision than on the communitarian ideal. Still, Boyte's stance is nuanced. He sees the possibility for parochial organizations nurturing generosity and cooperativeness that could eventually extend to a broader world. "Religious denominations, women's far-flung reform networks, networks of rural cooperatives, workers' organizations of self-help and mutual aid, to suggest a few examples, fit this pattern of locally grounded public spaces with larger reach."[44]

PARTICIPATORY COMMUNITY AS CAUTIOUS SEARCH FOR COOPERATIVE SMALL GROUPS. Jane Mansbridge is Robert Booth Fowler's spokesperson for a chastened, hedged form of participatory democracy, and an estimable representative she is. After being an admirer, or member, of a number of participatory groups (she mentions "free schools, food co-ops, law communes, women's centers, hot lines, and health clinics") she spent a decade studying such organizations and comparing them with the adversarial arrangements that characterize politics in the United States today.[45]

In the end, she concluded that participatory community does not present a model for an alternative form of national political life, saying, "Democracies as large as the modern nation-state [must] be primarily adversarial democracies. This is a bitter conclusion. It means rejecting the vision of national unitary democracy where interests coincide naturally, through unselfishness, or through the power of an idea." Her admiration for participatory community has not evaporated completely, but it is now complex and diminished. In egalitarian workplaces and small towns (each of which she has written about in case studies of participatory communities), "a citizen could learn the communal virtues, partake of a community of values, become a genuine participator in government." But even in the egalitarian workplace, commune, or neighborhood group, there will, on occasion, be serious differences on serious matters. Then the relation of friendship must, she concludes sadly, be replaced with the techniques of adversary democracy: leadership, representation, taking turns, and especially, voting. She advises that participatory communitarians "shift from unitary to adversary procedures and back again, depending on the goals they wish to pursue and the extent to which their members actually have interests in common."[46] Mansbridge's deep concern for the individual leads her to this conclusion. Otherwise the shyness of some members and skill of others might result in unstated reservations, frustrated intentions, imposed decisions, and false unity.

Mansbridge's moderated support for participatory community amounts to fond apostasy. She favors "revitalizing or creating institutions that foster a commitment to the common good." But she no longer sees the participatory community as an object of categorical commitment. She now perceives the family and the market, and thus all groups, to be predicated on "equally mixed motives,"[47] seemingly abandoning the argument that participatory community can be a repository of ultimate obligation and a font of consistently other-minded behavior.

### Mediating Community

In 1977 Peter L. Berger and Richard John Neuhaus wrote a gem of a book, *To Empower People: The Role of Mediating Structures in Public Policy*. Mediating structures are defined as those organizations between the individual and the "megastructures, . . . the large economic conglomerates of capitalist enterprise, big labor, and the growing bureaucracies . . . such as in education and the organized professions." Their message is encapsulated in two propositions: "Public policy should protect and foster mediating structures, and wherever possible, public policy should utilize mediating structures for the realization of social purposes."[48]

Their category, mediating structure, is broader than my term, mediating community. While their emphasis is on mediating, with the group functioning as a buffer and intervenor, mine is on community, viewing the group as the repository of commitment. Thus Berger and Neuhaus include neighborhoods and voluntary organizations along with families and religious organizations. The critical question here is to determine whether the ties within those organizations are strong enough to engender consistently other-minded behavior. Of course, for much of what we do we have mixed motives. Still, the degree to which self-interest influences our actions varies. Even Gary Becker, the University of Chicago economist who has made a career of predicting the behavior of people on the assumption that they act self-interestedly, acknowledges that "altruism dominates family behavior perhaps to the same extent that selfishness dominates market transactions."[49] Berger and Neuhaus implicitly acknowledge that neighborhoods and clubs have less of a hold on people than do family and religion, by including, when noting the variety of neighborhoods, those composed of people who welcome anonymity and lack of affiliation with others. These could hardly be called communities.

Recently a careful study attempted to determine the effects of neighborhood activity on civic involvement. The study concluded regretfully that even in those American cities that have created decentralized structures to involve citizens, "The data are unequivocal: overall participation is similar to that in the comparison groups. The [neighborhood] structures . . . do not bring people out of the woodwork."[50] Neighborhoods do not have the capacity to draw forth, with consistency, the intensity of sentiment found in families. However, there is no reason arbitrarily to exclude any type of organization from our set of those in which public purposes are accomplished when individuals look after others. Recall Boyte's finding, in some participatory communities, the capacity to generate public-spiritedness while focusing on parochial tasks. Any structure is a community if people in it are regularly drawn to seek the welfare of others.

We are looking for instances of such communities where people are so powerfully and consistently drawn to care for one another as to be better able to produce some services now turned over to government bureaus. My favorite example is Minnesota's family subsidy program. Some years ago while campaigning, I met a woman who described to me an experimental program in which her family was participating. She and her husband have a severely retarded son who had been living at government expense in a state hospital. The state had offered to pay them $200 a month (the stipend is now $250), if they wished to have their child live at home. They accepted the offer. They have used the money to fence in their backyard, to buy a helmet to protect their child's fragile head, and even to pay someone to look after the boy while they take an occasional weekend away from their exhausting chore. Here is an instance of state government's meeting a responsibility of a decent society, without going through a bureau but rather through a community—the family. Except perhaps for the public employees who previously attended the child, everyone is better off, including the taxpayers, whose cost has been cut by 90 percent. I successfully sponsored legislation to make the experimental program permanent.

James Coleman and Thomas Hoffer have made a case that another kind of mediating community, religious schools, can be similarly more efficacious than government institutions. (Their research base consisted of Catholic schools only because there are so few schools administered by other denominations. They appear to expect that the results they found in Catholic schools also hold in institutions operated by other religions.) Coleman and Hoffer found that compared with public school pupils—on each of whom, on average, society spends half again as much money—Catholic high school students have a strikingly lower dropout rate, make greater progress in the development of verbal and mathematical skills (though they apparently do no better in science and civics), and go on to college in larger numbers. Most impressively, "the achievement growth benefits of Catholic school attendance are especially strong for students who are in one way or other disadvantaged."[51]

Of course, it might be argued that the apparently superior ef-

fectiveness of religious schools is possibly due to differences between the parents who choose them and the parents of public
school children. Maybe the possibility that religious school parents, who take on added expense and obligations on behalf of
their children, also make the effort to provide an enriched home
life explains the relative educational success of their children.
Coleman and Hoffer were aware of that possibility. They determined, however, that the differential effects of religious schools
persist even after matching children as carefully as they could in
order to remove the possible effects of selection bias.[52] Recent research corroborates Coleman and Hoffer's rejection of selection
bias as the explanation for the difference in effectiveness between
public and religious schools. A more sophisticated study of the
effects of Catholic schools, by William N. Evans and Robert M.
Schwab, concludes "that for the typical student, attending a Catholic high school raises the probability of finishing high school or
entering a four-year college by 12 percentage points," and finds
"almost no evidence that the . . . estimates are subject to selection
bias."[53] Economist Derek Neal not only does not find positive selection bias, but conjectures that *negative* selection bias might be
present: "With respect to unobserved traits that enhance academic
performance, the best students from upper- and middle-class
homes may not be concentrated in Catholic schools but rather in
elite public schools." Neal also finds that "Catholic schooling
greatly increases educational attainment among urban minorities"
(particularly in their rate of graduation from high school). Furthermore, "minority students in urban Catholic schools can expect roughly 8 percent higher wages in the future simply because
they are more likely to complete high school and college."[54]

The selection bias issue also raises the question whether religious and other private schools are bringing a new segregation to
education as enclaves come together to educate only their kind.
In fact, however, middle-class flight from the major cities has left
public schools in inner cities all over America highly segregated.
On average, private schools in America are now less segregated
and are racially more representative of their communities than
are public schools. Indeed, private school students report more
cross-racial friendships than do public school students.[55]

That the religious schools' superior effectiveness is not attributable to their receiving more easily educated students is not surprising. Evidently, there is something in the school as community that provides superior education. For many children, especially the poorest of the poor, the devastating effects of fatherlessness can perhaps only be made up for (at least in part) by some form of community that bolsters the sustenance provided by overwhelmed mothers.[56] This possibility is made all the more important by the apparent fact that children not living with both parents suffer from living in less supportive neighborhoods. They move more often, which suggests weaker community ties, and their friends are more likely to be engaged in antisocial behavior.[57] Furthermore, one surmises that religious schools sometimes draw out from parents, as well as teachers, increased attentiveness to children's educational progress. Community brings forth altruism.

Anthony S. Bryk, Valerie E. Lee, and Peter B. Holland have reached similar conclusions concerning the effectiveness of (Catholic) schools that are communities.[58] Bryk and associates have identified a set of characteristics associated with superior performance in a school: demanding curriculum, high expectations of students, school-level decisionmaking, small size, and especially the school as a community. Invoking Jacques Maritain, the twentieth-century neo-scholastic philosopher, Bryk and associates contend that "democracy requires more than just a self-interested assent: students must come to love it and have a passion for it." Similarly, "those who teach the democratic charter must stake on it their personal convictions, their consciences, and the depths of their moral lives." Education divorced of conviction and morality becomes "a threat to the common good."[59] In other words, Catholic schools are effective because they are communities.

Others, including Nathan Glazer, and Paul Hill and his Rand Corporation associates, have also found that schools that are communities are more effective.[60] The Rand group wrote, "The conclusion is inescapable: Outcomes for disadvantaged students in focus schools exceeded those for the same students in [ordinary public] schools."[61] (Focus schools is the name given to both Catholic and "special-purpose" public schools. The two different kinds of focus school have several common features: they have clear missions, are strong organizations with authority to make and carry out many of their own policies, concentrate on student outcomes, and have contracts between student and school.) Within the category of focus school, the Catholic schools meet or exceed the quality of the special-purpose public schools on all of the measures used by the Hill group.

Coleman and Hoffer have a theory to explain the differential efficacy of religious schools. "The first prominent explanation for the difference is the functional community that exists around a religious body to which the families adhere and of which the school is an outgrowth." This is most clearly illustrated by the higher incidence of dropouts in public schools, which they understand as "induced by lack of social integration, either into a well-functioning and structurally intact family or into a close community." To Coleman and Hoffer, religious schools are especially effective in educating disadvantaged students, because, as an institution, they embody a particular form of community. Schools that are communities appear to some extent to be able to make up for "the decreased embeddedness of children and youth in family and community." Coleman and Hoffer conjecture that in religious schools deprived youngsters can evade the debilitating effects of being labeled as less educable. They see this as coming about partly because of "the egalitarian ethic of religion itself." Coleman and Hoffer recognize that while public schools can also be communities, in present-day America, when neighborhoods decreasingly are communities and when neighborhood schools are less common than in the past, that is unusual.[62] Religious schools tend more to be communities than do public schools.

Evidence of the efficacy of mediating communities is most abundant in the case of schools, but additional research on communities is proliferating and is showing that religious communities, in particular, appear to be successful in carrying out a variety of other services for which state governments have accepted responsibility. For example, African American churches show signs of remarkable effectiveness in drug rehabilitation.[63] Though for a time criminologists were skeptical of religion's positive effect on criminal behavior, recent research does find such a relationship.[64]

Church attendance and participation in church-based programs are associated with an improved sense of well-being among persons suffering from physical health problems and with greatly decreased dropout rates from school, decreased use of drugs, and diminished rates of engagement in other illegal behavior.[65] Children whose neighbors go to church regularly are less likely to be in trouble with the law, less likely to take drugs, and more likely to be employed.[66] There is some small evidence that not-for-profit nursing homes (many of them religious) are of higher quality than are for-profit homes.[67] Changing government's reimbursement rules for medicare and medicaid could permit many persons now in nursing homes to be cared for at less cost at home or in community facilities.[68] These are not isolated examples. Michael J. Donahue and Peter L. Benson, summarizing the literature on the relationship between religiousness and adolescent well-being, conclude: "Religiousness is positively associated with prosocial values and behavior, and negatively related to suicide ideation and attempts, substance abuse, premature sexual involvement, and delinquency. . . . These results are robust after controlling for sociodemographic characteristics."[69]

There is considerable dispute among academicians concerning whether the apparent altruism of monks, spouses, parents, and other mediating community members ultimately emerges from self-interest or reflects an other-mindedness inherent in understanding oneself as a member of a community. Coleman himself invoked rational choice theory and its economic method to try to explain the formation of communities. He referred to the intimate relationships that characterize communities as social capital. He thought this social capital to be influenced greatly by the impossibility of using money as a form of exchange.[70] In a family, making the bed, mowing the lawn, and reading to the children are not activities performed in exchange for money. Coleman saw those ordinary activities and expectations of family life as the reasonable responses of self-interested persons to a situation in which money payments are impractical. Patterns of reciprocity in kind become built into family life. He called those patterns, or norms, social capital. He and Thomas Hoffer contended that similar social capital develops in some schools. Coleman and Hoffer referred to social capital as having positive external benefits. A parent volunteering at a school helps other children besides his own. A nun, whose vows bind her night and day to her mission of teaching, will bring benefits to her students for which she is not compensated. The environment and norms in a community are public goods largely created by persons (parents in a family, teachers and parents in a school) who are not themselves the main beneficiaries and who are not compensated in relation to their contributions. William C. Mitchell, in a sympathetic review of the state of the new economics of organization, admits that the new discipline has not yet been able to accommodate altruism.[71]

To me it is clear that some associations engender altruism, but I will proceed on the basis that it is not necessary to resolve the question whether people in communities are truly altruistic. For policy purposes we are less interested in motives than effects. There are organizations in which societal responsibilities are carried out better, or less expensively, than in bureaus or firms because, for whatever reason, people in them are drawn to help one another. For most people, perhaps only family and religion constitute community, but the society also benefits when other groups generate consistent other-mindedness.[72] Community becomes a possible instrument of policy because in a community people ordinarily act in ways that are beneficial to others; they need less inducement, compensation, supervision, and monitoring.

Communities are fragile. It requires no great leap to surmise that in many or all mediating communities, starting with families and religious organizations, there is a good deal of selfish behavior. And mediating communities can be repressive. Amartya Sen notes that "valuing the cohesion of the family in many gender-unequal societies can actually serve to perpetuate the unequal position of women, by making women themselves give priority to the alleged interest of the family over personal well-being."[73] Yet, though there are exceptions, patterns of community efficacy persist. While on one level this is controversial, at another it is obvious and inescapable. Most "social services" engaged in by the states (child care, the tending of the infirm, and even much education) are performed within mediating communities without compensation and without anyone thinking they are producing a service. Mary Ann Glendon writes, "Families are still the major means through which society deals with persons who are not independent." However, she continues, "in our time, by promoting individual rights at the expense of nearly every other social value in family law, labor law, and constitutional law, we have deprived families, churches, and other forms of fellowship of some of their mutually sustaining influences."[74] It is within mediating communities that we are formed; therein lie our ultimate loyalties. Perhaps only there can we learn civic-mindedness and concern for others, including those outside the small community.[75] Of course communities sometimes fail. Like markets and governments, they are composed of humans. But they contain and engender more persistent other-mindedness than do markets and governments. Besides producing services, they nurture and protect us all, they cut costs of getting things done, create social capital, obviate the need for some government services, and engender civic virtue.

It is the possibility of consistent altruism that distinguishes the organizations here called mediating communities. Economists have attempted to explain the behavior of some nonprofit organizations without invoking altruism. They point to the "nondistribution constraint"—the requirement that owners and employees of a not-for-profit organization cannot benefit financially by causing the organization's revenues to exceed its costs.[76] They note that the nondistribution constraint can generate trust among clients. This constraint can be especially helpful in cases where recipients of a good or service find it hard to measure its quality, as well as cases where producers possess more information about a product than do recipients. The constraint might inhibit attempts on the part of producers to use the recipients' lack of information to reap benefits at their expense, because it removes a monetary advantage from doing so. This explanation for why nonprofits exist and how they operate makes no reference to the possibility that in some circumstances people are not inclined to take advantage of information asymmetries; indeed they may actively seek to help recipients of services rather than bilk them.

Family, religion, and other mediating communities are not to be construed merely as instruments of government. To members they are dear beyond price, and their manipulation by government can constitute profanation. One simple way out of this difficulty would be to eschew the use of community as policy. But a central theme of this book is the inherent inadequacy of bureaus and the insufficiency of firms when it comes to producing necessary goods and services. Community will be an indispensable instrument of policy, so vigilance to guard its integrity must be a necessary part of private and public life.

## Conclusion

Community is a nebulous and theoretically disputed phenomenon. Construing a state, or the whole of the country, as a community has to be recognized as a lovely aspiration—certainly one to be encouraged, but not one that is realistic for policy purposes. Mediating communities are smaller organizations in which people, at least somewhat consistently, look out for the welfare of others, and their efficacy in so doing is what distinguishes the argument made in this book from inclusive communitarianism, on the one hand, and the economists' explanation of organizational behavior, on the other.

We have seen that there are cases where groups of people in mediating communities are dependably drawn to help others in ways that meet governmental responsibilities. The two reasons that community could become a possible instrument of policy and a potential source of efficiency and innovation are that communities can inspire effort and creativity and they can get by with lower costs for management and oversight. Community becomes the only alternative to competition as a means of accomplishing a patterned coincidence of individual and societal interests.

States now expend most of their budgets on services produced by bureaus. The states might be facing a stark choice: either paying mediating communities to perform many governmental responsibilities now being carried out in bureaus, or become resigned to inadequate services.

# 7

## *Competition and Community: Policies for the States*

THIS CHAPTER rests on and applies the argument made above, that only two strong, persistently efficacious, and largely self-regulating means exist for carrying out most of the responsibilities of state government: competition and community. Effective delivery of public services is more than bestowing money and bright ideas on able public employees. It involves more than the talented efforts and noble declarations of leaders and managers. Effective policy must contain incentive or inspiration to accomplish a public purpose. Little such incentive or inspiration pervades the vast apparatuses through which state governments now try to provide education and health care and to fulfill their other responsibilities.

Other policy instruments, especially the standard ones—appropriations, exhortations, and mandates—often lack efficacy if applied in the absence of the steady orientation toward achieving public purposes that is provided by competition and community. Restructuring the delivery of government services means designing choice and community directly into policies. Hope for better government in the future rests on restructuring, so defined. The arguments for competition and community are not airtight, but they have theoretical and empirical underpinnings in their favor. The success of other policies depends on spontaneous good will

115

or on omnipresent and benevolent political oversight, which, unfortunately, is simply not always dependable.[1]

## Using Competition

Since the great bulk of state government spending ultimately goes to funding the production of services, the following discussion is limited to that topic. A general policy of competition would be broader. For example, governments can, and sometimes do, use competitive bidding to allocate rights to fishing, water, forest harvesting, and airwaves, as well as permits to pollute. Only minor adjustments would be required to adapt the following discussion for application to those other items.

Lately government-designed competitive arrangements for fostering innovation, efficiency, and self-policing in the production of services have come to be called *social markets*.[2] In describing the five elements in the design of a social market, I will use state government's main responsibility, elementary and secondary education, as the primary illustration.

### Citizens Choose from among Potential Suppliers of Service

On one level the idea of citizens choosing their service producer is bromidic. Americans are accustomed to making many decisions for themselves. But for some public services, in particular elementary and secondary education, we have long accepted assignment by government authorities. Students might have some choice within their school district, but few in America are permitted to attend a public school outside their home district. To defend the currently widespread policy of denial of choice would require demonstrating that it yields satisfactory results. Chapters 3 and 4 refute that argument by demonstrating the inadequacy of the current arrangement of school districts organized and operating as territorial monopoly bureaus. Choice is as necessary for innovative and efficient public services as for any of the plethora of privately produced goods and services in this country. At this time there is no persuasive defense of the bureaucratic monopolies of the states, no plausible theory that would lead one to expect consistently acceptable quality from them.

There are two parts to this first element of a policy of competition: citizens, not government officials, must be able to choose the producer from which they will receive a service; and there must be a variety of potential producers from which to choose. The power of competitive markets to foster innovation and efficiency is due to these two factors. The recipient, as the party experiencing the service, can be expected to seek superior results. The multitude of producers, under continual pressure to vie for sales, devise product improvements and offer them at the best price they can. The intensely competitive computer industry illustrates this point: immense improvements in computer technology are occurring nearly daily, with a simultaneous decline in prices. School districts, organized as territorial monopoly bureaus, are protected from that kind of competition. They are funded whether or not they perform.

Social markets embody these forces. Since the basic problem we are trying to overcome is waste, diversion, or other abuse by people with power, it is preferable for the ultimate recipients of the services—students and their families, in the case of education—to make the purchasing decisions. They themselves bear the effects of the services, whereas public officials are a step removed; government employees spend other people's money for the presumed benefit of still others. Behind a social market is the notion that ordinarily the recipients of services are more concerned about, and better judges of, their needs than is anyone in government.

However, recipients of a service might not express all of society's relevant interests. Government frequently provides services because of flaws in private markets. Some of these occur where a service has effects, deleterious or beneficial, on others besides the recipient. As we saw in chapter 4, externalities are not necessarily and automatically accounted for in a market. If benefits accrue to others in addition to the person learning to read or being vaccinated, leaving education or health care entirely in the hands of private enterprise might result in inadequate amounts of these services. In addition, society might wish to require, through its government, that certain subject matter be included in school curricula or that minimum levels of health care be available to all. Another instance of recipients not expressing society's preferences occurs in the case of public goods. A public good—such as police protection, research, or the services of a lighthouse—is one that if enjoyed by one person is entirely available for others. Economists have long noted that many people will not step forward to purchase such a good; they will, however, wait for others to do so, and then enjoy the good without paying for it, as "free riders." It is not as simple as leaving services to be taken care of by private markets or even having services funded by government but produced by private organizations and purchased by private citizens. Such a hands-off approach by government could potentially leave market failures in place. Thus there will be times when government officials must make the choice of producer. When they do so, however, the second element of a social market is necessary.

### Splitting Purchaser and Producer

A conflict of interest exists when the entity that buys a good or service (especially when it does so with other people's money) also produces and sells it. As a buyer this entity can hardly be expected to search among potential sellers for the best bargain, and as a seller assured of a buyer, it is less likely to hold down costs and seek to improve the quality of the product.

In this regard, a curious blind spot prevails in America. It would be easy for all to see a conflict of interest were government to purchase all its automobiles from a monopoly it owns, or were it to buy paper or foodstuff in that way. (Such arrangements were the source of the inefficiency, lack of innovativeness, and ultimately the collapse of the communist economies.) But that is the arrangement used by the states to fund and produce a variety of public services. Prisons, state hospitals, and, most significantly, elementary and secondary education are organized in this fashion. A school board has an exclusive franchise to produce public education in its jurisdiction. It also pays all the bills, being the sole purchaser of the education. The ultimate recipients of education, students and their families, however, have difficulty influencing the producer. In comparison with employees of the schools, students and their parents are relatively poorly politically organized, and, as they have little market power, are able to exert scant influence. Those, however, who work in the government agencies that produce services, especially teachers, are highly organized. Their positions carry considerable weight in the state capitols, where they purport to speak on behalf of the students. It is puzzling that citizens accept this arrangement. When a chairman of the country's largest auto maker declared that what's good for General Motors is good for the country, the public's derision endured for decades. But when teachers—and I am one—contend that their students' interests coincide with their own, there is surprisingly little public questioning of the claim.

If purchaser and producer were split in education, school boards would engage in arm's-length contracting for purchase of educational services from schools they do not own, as was described in the discussion of charter schools in chapter 5.

A purchaser-producer split is as necessary for publicly produced services as for those produced privately.[3] If school boards retain responsibility for producing services, then their policymaking and funding responsibilities are compromised. As currently organized, the provision of services by the states is rife with conflicts of interest.

It is not feasible for all service choices to be made by individual citizen-recipients. While government officials will have to make some choices, that number should be held to a minimum. The more decisions made by people for the presumed benefit of others, the more opportunities for slack, mischief, and self-aggrandizement. When government officials make service choices, the primary protection against abuse and inefficiency is a purchaser-producer split.

## Debureaucratization

The first two elements of a social market imply the need for the third one, debureaucratization, which means that government organizations that produce services are to be financed not by lump-sum transfers from legislatures, but on a contractual basis from people who choose their services.

The innovation- and efficiency-inducing character of markets arises not from their being private, but from the dynamic generated by the existence of many suppliers whose revenues depend, crucially, on satisfied recipients of their good or service. In chapter 4 we saw that only rarely and episodically does one find bureaus subjected to consistently efficacious oversight and management. This may be inevitable under our form of government in which interest groups may influence the design of bureaucratic arrangements concerning them so as to remove themselves from careful scrutiny. If a supplier is funded as a bureau, meaning by a sponsoring legislature rather than by sales to recipients, the invigorating dynamic is missing. There may then be little inducement to be responsive and even less requirement to be innovative or efficient. Where feasible, social markets eliminate lump-sum financing from bureaus and transform them into organizations that are financed to the extent that they can persuade willing citizen-recipients to pay for their services.

Debureaucratization in education would see parents, on the one hand, and school boards, on the other, contracting with schools for stipulated performance in exchange for payment.

Still, competitive social markets will not be entirely self-regulatory. Presumably government is involved because some factor important to society is not being considered by private buyers and sellers. Consequently social markets require additional features to ensure that public purposes are met. A fourth and a fifth element are necessary features of a policy of competition.

### Explicit Provision for Attainment of Social Objectives

The difference between private and social markets lies in the fact that in social markets society has relevant interests not necessarily considered by either recipient or supplier. Means for achieving the objectives need to be incorporated into government's policy. Government has two main ways to achieve this: make attainment of the objectives a condition of participation in the social market, or implement a tax or subsidy that provides an incentive for attaining the goals. For example, government might settle on an objective that each school reflect society's racial or aptitude diversity, and, as a condition for receiving funding, require that schools admit all students who apply or admit them by lot from the applicant pool. Similarly, out of concern that schools not be segregated by income, government might require that in order to participate in a voucher program, schools would have to accept the government's voucher as full payment (even if it is less than a school's costs). Or government might grant a larger voucher for students who are hard to teach. Societal considerations will arise, ones not necessarily entering the calculations of service recipients, requiring government action to design social markets to accomplish those public purposes.

### Independent Monitoring

To some extent, a market is a substitute for measurement of results. No one needs to put a gauge on you to determine whether the broccoli you bought and ate yesterday satisfied you. Often a person's having freely chosen to make a purchase is sufficient evidence that it is satisfactory to that individual. Obviously, however, there are many goods for which consumers do not know all the effects—effects on themselves, as well as those on others. For this reason, and because in social markets goals other than those of the recipients may be relevant, there ordinarily needs to be a monitoring entity to inform recipients, government officials, and the general public of the effects of the various producers. This information will permit comparisons among service producers to facilitate selection of superior providers. In general, monitoring is best carried out by organizations without a stake in the findings. It is asking for trouble to have monitoring conducted by organizations, such as school boards, with an interest in the results.

In sum, a properly designed social market embodies the features that orient competitive private markets toward efficiency, innovation, and self-policing—numerous sellers vying for the favor of buyers who are at arm's length from them. When those choosing the services are public officials, production should not also be in their hands. A social market also includes independent monitoring and, sometimes, additional precautions imposed by government.

## The Three Kinds of Competition-Inducing Policies

The above discussion implies that there are three broad kinds of policies to foster competition where government finances service production: place choice in the hands of citizen-recipients, ensure a variety of choices of producer, and, when choice by citizens is not feasible, adopt choice by public officials. The first vests market demand in the hands of citizens; the second protects against monopoly in supply. If either of those two is neglected, competition is undermined. The third type of policy incorporates a purchaser-producer split when government officials, rather than citizens, choose. The three are shown in table 7-1. Items in parentheses are examples of legislation that would accomplish the respective policies for elementary and secondary education.

Table 7-2 shows how social markets respond to the market and government failures identified in chapter 4 as the explanation for the current inadequate quality of services provided by state gov-

### Table 7-1. Three Policies for Introducing Competition into the Production of Services Provided by Government[a]

*Place choice in the hands of citizen-recipients*
>    Permit choice from among government producers (open enrollment)
>    Allot capitation payments to citizen-recipients (vouchers or credits)*

*Ensure a variety of choices*
>    Government producers
>        Permit choice from among government producers other than current
>            producers (open enrollment, charter schools)
>        Allot capitation payments to qualified producers (site-based funding)
>    Government or private producers
>        Permit choice from among government or private producers
>            (vouchers or credits)*

*Establish choice for government officials*
>        Institutionalize competitive bidding for service production (school
>            boards contract with government or private entitites for production
>            of educational services)

* Policies that combine both competition and community (see discussion in text).
a. Examples from elementary and secondary education.

ernments. Recall that the items listed in the left column of table 7-2 are the ways that private and public organizations fail because people are not oriented to act in socially beneficial fashion. Each entry in the other two columns embodies one or more of the elements of a social market. In each case, properly structured competition orients individuals to behave in a fashion that undoes or prevents the corresponding organizational failure. Competition corrects much market and government failure.

## Using Community

The case to be made for community production of government-financed services is less straightforward than is the case for competition, because community does not embody a mechanism akin to that long recognized in the operation of competition. Nevertheless, the American tradition of, and penchant for, individual choice, the bankruptcy of bureaucratic production as discussed in chapters 3 and 4, and the empirical evidence of the efficacy of communities as described in chapter 6, all point to the appropriateness of a large-scale shift by the states from bureaus to communities for the production of a variety of services. There are five elements in a policy of using communities.

### Indirect Government Finance

For several reasons, indirect finance, with the government-subsidized recipient choosing the service producer rather than the government doing so, is preferable to direct contracting between government and community producer. Burton Weisbrod cites government's rigidity, its disinclination to offer or select a variety of services corresponding to the variety of recipient preferences, as justification for this preference.[4] At times, there may be merit in doing without a service altogether. John McKnight argues that professional service providers can become intrusive and could even contribute to debilitation in recipients who, unless care is taken, can begin to see themselves as deficient and in perpetual need of the ministrations of the professional server.[5] "The helping hand strikes again," is Robert Woodson's wry de-

**Table 7-2. Designs for Policymaking: Competition as a Response to Market and Government Failure**[a]

| Organizational failure | Competitive responses | |
|---|---|---|
| | *Individuals choose* | *Government officials choose* |
| *Lack of salutary external orientation* | | |
| Monopoly | Government grants authority to additional producers (eliminate territorial monopoly of school boards) | Government purchases by competitive bid (school boards choose from education producers) |
| | | Government allocates franchises by auction (school boards choose from education producers) |
| Bureaucratic production | Government finances producing organizations per capita (state funds not districts but schools families choose) | Government purchases by competitive bid (see above) |
| Public goods or externalities | Government taxes or subsidizes (vouchers encourage education) | Government purchases by competitive bid (see above) |
| *Lack of salutary internal orientation* | | |
| Internalities | Monitors inform recipients, citizenry, policymakers (testing of results permits comparison of schools and districts) | Monitors inform recipients, citizenry, policymakers (testing of results permits comparison of schools and districts) |
| Income maldistribution | Government grants vouchers, refundable tax credits (funds permit choice by families of their children's school) | Government contracts through competitive bid for services to be provided to disadvantaged persons (schools and boards contract for services for needy children) |

a. Examples from elementary and secondary education.

scription of this phenomenon.[6] A related danger in direct contracting is excessive entanglement between government and religious institutions. These several concerns can be summarized in the observation that communities can rarely be imposed by government but depend, rather, on the commitment of individuals. (Of course, for the situations when recipient choice is infeasible, government will contract directly with a community, as in the care of orphans or mentally impaired persons, or custodianship over prisoners.)

Now, even their champions recognize that communities can be flawed, can go awry. Peter Berger and Richard John Neuhaus, the most persuasive proponents of governments acting through communities, concede that "strictly speaking . . . the Mafia, the Ku Klux Klan . . . could also be described as mediating structures." They assert that "the beliefs and values thus mediated are criminal, immoral, or plain crazy" and conclude that precautions need to be taken to prevent inadvertent government support of such organizations.[7] Michael Sandel has the same reservations: "To accord the political community a stake in the character of its citizens is to concede the possibility that bad communities may form bad characters. Dispersed power and multiple sites of civic formation may reduce the dangers but cannot remove them." Still, he argues that such risks are inherent in a pluralist society. He goes further, turning the objection around to maintain that politics and bureaucracies, both often rule-driven and devoid of public-spiritedness, "cannot secure the liberty [they promise], because [they] cannot inspire the moral and civic engagement self-government requires." And, "even a realized welfare state cannot secure the part of freedom bound up with sharing in self-rule; it cannot provide, and may very well even erode, the civic capacities and communal resources necessary to self-government."[8] My thesis is that it is necessary to use communities in order to get the work done. Sandel contends persuasively that, apart from this instrumental consideration, unless communities thrive, the civic virtue required for democratic politics cannot be developed and sustained.

Communities will be necessary but, so too, will be precautions concerning them.

## A Nondistribution Constraint

As explained in chapter 6, the value of a constraint requiring the nondistribution of profits lies in its encouragement of probity by organizations, and thus trust in those organizations. The more difficult it is to measure service quality and the less observable the processes of production, the more appropriate is the nondistribution constraint. Since owners and employees of the organizations subject to this constraint cannot retain profits for themselves, they might be more inclined than otherwise to work for the public purpose of the organizations, that is, for government-stipulated societal objectives not necessarily held by either purchaser or producer. Further, an organization that cannot thrive under such a constraint is unlikely to constitute a community. So this first precaution, the nondistribution constraint, should be understood both as an encouragement and as a hurdle. The constraint has a downside: forbidding profit removes profit's incentive to innovate and to operate efficiently. If that incentive is not replaced by the zeal and altruism of a true community, there may be no reason to turn to nonprofits. Also, recipients of government funds for services might spend them within their own families (as is allowed with Minnesota's family subsidy program, described in chapter 6). This is inconsistent with a purchaser-producer split and thus could elicit concern that the funds will not be used so as to encourage economizing and innovation. For these reasons, further precautions are required to ensure that the organizations to which individuals (with government funds) turn for services are indeed communities.

## Underfunding

Producing organizations will object, but a policy of resorting to communities entails providing less government funding than might be necessary for purchase from a bureau or a private firm. This is not intended to punish, or even to stimulate efficiency, but rather to ensure that producers are in fact communities, with members inspired enough to be willing to work for less than similarly situated people in for-profit organizations. As I say, they will object. But we are concerned here with services—education, medical care, attending to the infirm—where measurement of results is difficult and where there are opportunities to take shortcuts. Forcing communities that receive government funds to scrimp is a way that society discerns their authenticity.

The two remaining elements of a policy of community are the same as the final two elements of a policy of competition: explicit provision for attainment of social objectives over and above those of the citizen-recipients and independent monitoring.[9]

## The Complementarity of Competition and Community

What strikes one most when studying the policies of competition and community is their complementarity. America does not decide between competition and community, individuality and associativeness, but rather embraces both. In our time, this Tocquevillian point has been most clearly seen and forcefully expounded by Michael Novak, who goes so far as to write, "The very structure of democratic capitalism—even its impersonal economic system—is aimed at community . . . the community of free persons in voluntary association." Novak relishes calling Americans "communitarian individuals."[10]

Several of the elements of the two policies are identical. The two policies have the following in common:

—Both replace bureaus with organizations dependent on satisfied recipients for their resources.

—In both, persons choose services from among a variety of potential producers.

—Both sometimes require explicit provision for meeting societal objectives over and above those of producers and recipients.

—Both require independent monitoring because recipients, purchasers, and producers might not, among them, hold some of the relevant societal objectives, and thus might not work to meet those objectives unless subject to monitoring.

There are differences between the two policies:

—They depend on different, though sometimes compatible, motive forces. Competition requires some virtue in its participants, but its power comes from the combination of the profit motive and the requirement to satisfy customers in order to stay in existence. Markets do not depend on altruism; communities do.

—Because of the difference in motive forces, a policy of competition requires a purchaser-producer split, but a policy of community does not. Indeed, sometimes a community will reject purchase of service as inappropriate and will provide the equivalent of service itself (as when a family educates its own children or cares for infirm loved ones).

Noticing the complementarity of choice and community helps one to identify a mistake sometimes made by persons attempting to describe how competition works. "All choice plans," writes Thomas J. Kane, "rely upon exit, or the threat of exit, as the primary means of sending the message to schools to improve."[11] Not necessarily. In this book I have shown the possibility of choosing community, that is, choosing to be the beneficiary, as well as the practitioner, of altruism. Choice can foster loyalty and industry. It is not at all clear that the primary means by which schools improve when they are chosen is the threat of exit.

Much of state policymaking comes down to the provision of services through the policies of competition and community. Since the policies depend on somewhat different motive forces, in any particular application it is necessary to determine which of the two is expected to bring about the desired result, then to put in place the elements of that policy.

Table 7-2 yields an important observation. It shows competitive policies divided between those in which individual citizens choose a service producer and those in which government officials choose. The point to be made here is that all of the competitive responses in the column labeled "Individuals Choose" are consistent with a policy of community. That is, when government resorts to subsidizing individuals to enter a competitive market for services, the possibility exists for both competitive pressures and community inspiration to work toward innovative and efficient services.

Thus it can now be seen that table 7-1 amalgamates both competition and community. Policies there marked with an asterisk incorporate both competition and community; those not marked use competition alone.

## Choice and Community: An Agenda for the States

An agenda of choice and community for the provision of most state services incorporates three main policies: authorization for citizens to choose service providers; ensuring that choices exist for them; and, if citizen choice is infeasible, having government officials choose. Several precautions protect against bureaucratization and against organizations that falsely present themselves as communities: indirect funding, nondistribution of profits, underfunding, a provider-producer split, explicit provision for social objectives to be met, and independent monitoring. In table 7-3, the culmination of the argument of this book, I outline a variety of applications of the argument to some of the large responsibilities of state government. Its left column displays the three policies from table 7-2 that incorporate competition and community. The body illustrates those policies as applied to several of the main objects of state government expenditure: elementary and secondary education, health care, higher education, corrections, and aid to local governments. The latter item is included to show that even though the thesis of the book is intended to apply to the provision of services, it can also apply to other activities of state government, including distribution of funds. For each substantive area of policy shown in table 7-3, if one or more of the applications appearing there are not implemented, one might ask how then are favorable results expected to be achieved?

Note that the elements of an agenda of choice and community are already in place in higher education more than in any other area. Most observers would say that, for all its faults, higher education is in better condition than are any other of the major responsibilities of state government.

From table 2-1 (see page 18), we can see that little current state government spending now takes place in competitive or community arrangements. Column B shows that only about one-sixth of what states now do takes place in social markets. The major service that falls into column B, higher education, is "sold" to students, but the quotation marks remind the reader that recipients of public higher education typically pay, in tuition and fees, far less than half the cost of their education. Another one-sixth

**Table 7-3. Using Competition and Community to Accomplish the Main Responsibilities of State Government**

| Policies | Type of program and applications | | | | |
| --- | --- | --- | --- | --- | --- |
| | Elementary and secondary education | Higher education | Health care | Corrections | Aid to local governments |
| *Choice by citizen-recipients* | | | | | |
| From among government producers | Open enrollment (families choose any public school in any school district) | Open enrollment (students choose their college) | Open enrollment (persons choose their health plan) | ... | State aid not to local governments but to needy individuals |
| From among government or private producers | Vouchers, tax credits (government funds go not to school boards but to families, which spend them at the school they choose) | Vouchers, tax credits (state funds go to students instead of to colleges) | Medical savings accounts (vouchers to individuals, perhaps combined with catastrophic insurance) | ... | ... |
| *A variety of choices ensured* | | | | | |
| Among government producers | Charter schools (schools owned by government entities other than school boards, which operate only as long as they achieve specified results) | Charter universities (public colleges that operate under contract only as long as they achieve specified results) | Charter hospitals (public facilities that operate under contract only as long as they achieve specified results) | ... | State aid not to local governments but to needy individuals |

| | | | | | |
|---|---|---|---|---|---|
| *Among government or private producers* | Capitated, site-based funding (funds go not to school boards but to schools on the basis of enrollment)<br><br>Vouchers, tax credits (families choose their school, public or private) | Site-based funding (state funds go to colleges on the basis of numbers of students who have chosen to enroll)<br><br>Vouchers, tax credits | Site-based funding (state funds go to medical facilities on the basis of numbers of persons who have chosen them)<br><br>Medical savings accounts | ⋮<br><br>⋮ | |
| *Choice for government officials* | School boards, perhaps divested of ownership of schools, contract with public or private entities for services | Colleges contract with their employees and with private entities for services | Government contracts with public or private entities for services | Government contracts with public or private organizations for custodianship of prisoners | Local governments bid for contracts from state governments |

of current spending (column F) is transferred to individuals, but almost none of this is in the form of vouchers to be used for purchase of services. Rather, it is almost all mere transfer of funds, mostly pensions and insurance. A policy of competition and community would see funds transferred from columns A, C, and D, where most money is now going (that is, most state production of services is bureaucratic; there nothing is given as a quid pro quo for government's funds or services, and communities are hardly encouraged). Under an agenda of competition and community, most state spending would flow into columns B and, especially, E. Government would sell more services and would grant funds to citizen-recipients to enable them to choose services for themselves.

Of course, not all of state government's responsibilities, not even all of its services, fit into an agenda of choice and community. (The blank spaces under "Corrections" in table 7-3 testify to the foolishness of letting prisoners choose their facility.) However, much of what is now done through bureaus can be profitably switched, leaving policymakers free to focus on those items of government requiring their attention. And while ultimately there is no getting around the necessity of virtue among public officials, to depend on it when it is not necessary seems senseless. There also remains the possibility that even while necessary, virtue is best developed in communities, another reason for turning to the agenda offered in this book.

## Conclusion

An agenda of choice and community would not necessarily change the responsibilities of state governments, but it would change dramatically the ways in which they go about meeting them. To this day the states rely largely on monopoly production by government-owned bureaus. Using competition and community would entail:

—More state money flowing from government to individuals, with less to school boards, colleges, and cities;

—Meeting many of state government's responsibilities through communities rather than through government-owned bureaus;

—Submitting governmental, as well as private service, producers to competition; and, in general,

—Constituting government as arranger, funder, and monitor, but not necessarily as producer, of services.

For the states, the lessons of our time are that government has major responsibilities to its citizens, that when government operates through bureaus it frequently fails in the fulfillment of its purposes, and that two alternatives to bureaus—competition and communities—offer promise of better meeting those responsibilities.

# 8

# *Reprise*

S TATE GOVERNMENTS are entering a difficult period. The economy continues to grow more slowly than it did for the period from the Civil War to the 1970s, and citizens are no longer accepting increases in the portion of income going to taxes. Meanwhile, state spending is concentrated on the production of a handful of services, each important to the society's well-being. The largest of these expenditures (education and medical care) and the fastest growing (corrections) are all experiencing rapidly expanding, demographically driven demands. Because revenue growth will be lower and demand growth higher than in the past, there is no practical possibility that the huge increases, of recent decades, in spending per student and per patient will continue.

Furthermore, the immense budget increases of the states have not yielded correspondingly better results in the provision of services. The weightiest finding of policy evaluation in our time is that, on average, only a weak relationship exists between the amount of money spent and results achieved for much of what government does. The budget, often called the embodiment of policy, is, in fact, a feeble instrument.

Throughout much of this century, influential theories of economics and public administration conveyed the reassuring impression that when private markets fail, government policymakers stand ready to take corrective actions, with capable civil servants prepared to faithfully carry out those policies. These misleading theories shored up the erroneous notion that government spending would automatically yield hoped-for results. A still-emerging new economics of organization, which has been developing for several decades, explains why much current policy fails. This new social science attributes to politicians and bureaucrats the same self-interested behavior that economists ascribe to private entrepreneurs (who are assumed to maximize profits) and consumers (who are assumed to maximize their own satisfaction). In the new economics of organization, politicians and bureaucrats are understood as characteristically seeking perquisites of office. Up to now, state governments' policies have hardly been affected by the new economics.

This extension of the discipline of economics is also an extension of James Madison's understanding that governments, at times, fail for the same reason that markets, at times, fail: because some people sometimes take advantage of others. Monopolies, public and private, are unresponsive and gouging. Bureaus tend, inherently, to clumsiness and waste. Externalities, such as pollution, are inflicted on society by governments, as well as by private organizations, because the perpetrators are not held liable for the costs incurred by their actions. Information asymmetries permit politicians and bureaucrats, as well as private sector entrepreneurs and managers, to gain undeserved benefits for themselves. Market failure yields inefficiency and unfairness. Government failure yields inefficiency and unfairness.

The new economics also identifies a defect of much policy research. In recent times, vast sums have been expended on evaluations and experiments seeking to determine "what works" in public policy. Much has been learned about what characterizes effective schools, welfare programs, and other government activities. The unexamined presumption behind the policy research was that the knowledge it produced would be put to use, while, in fact, much of it has been ignored. Giving people information about how to be more productive does not mean they will use that information. We do not necessarily put into action what we know works.

Much advice concerning public management has been of little value for the same reason that much policy research has been useless. Consultants have recommended that managers employ this or that decision system (such as zero-based budgeting or management by objectives), or resort to total quality management, or cut out layers of bureaucracy, or otherwise take actions that would seem to be in the public interest. But to urge is not to compel. One reason for the existence of government is the fact that people often take undeserved benefits at the expense of others. It cannot be assumed that people, including public managers, will automatically seek the public interest and employ the most effective management techniques that have been pressed on them. Naturally, those who work for the government need information as to the best means to accomplish public purposes. But of prior, and far greater, importance is their receptivity to this advice, their orientation to want to act in ways that accomplish public purposes.

The new economics of organization not only provides an explanation for the failure of state government to produce consistently satisfactory services, for the lack of influence of much policy research, and for the limitations of public management; it also points the way to the design of more effective policy. Policymaking has heretofore been understood as priority setting and budget allocation. This conception of policymaking has been discredited by the fact that neither stipulating priorities nor distributing money necessarily produces hoped-for results. Since both market failure and government failure come about when individuals advance their own interests at the expense of others, policy is unlikely to succeed unless it arranges incentives so that when persons act in their own interests, they also meet public purposes.

At first blush, the foregoing might suggest widespread manipulation of incentives by those in authority. Some kinds of behavior could be discouraged and others encouraged by adjusting prices up or down, by levying taxes, or by implementing subsidies. Polluters can be hit with a tax equal to the cost their pollution imposes on the rest of society. This presumably impels the polluters, acting in their own interests, to cut back on the problems they create. Similarly, research, schooling, and other activities thought to have societywide benefits are encouraged when their prices are reduced through subsidies. Such a policy of adjusting prices induces individuals, acting in their own interests, to meet public purposes. Society benefits when government more carefully aligns incentives. But here is the catch: government policymakers cannot be expected, any more than others, to act consistently with the good of society in mind. While a thoroughgoing policy of influencing behavior by altering prices should be part of a government's repertoire, it should be resorted to sparingly, for it can possess a fatal flaw—those devising the policy might not be acting in the public interest. The effect of this flaw has vividly emerged in recent years as we have witnessed its contribution to the colossal failure of communist regimes. Incompetent and corrupt price setting by central governments in those countries fostered inefficiency and slow economic growth, leading to overall failure.

Is there any *self-policing* arrangement that brings private and public interests into correspondence? As both Adam Smith and James Madison saw, in a free society of people expected to act in their own self-interest, competition—the institutionalization of countervailing forces—provides this function. In markets and politics, competition both engenders innovation and at the same time constrains people from taking advantage of others. The prospect of profit stimulates creativity and industry, but excessive profits are whittled away when competitors enter a market. In politics, competing interest groups (Madison called them "factions") sometimes discipline each other. Competition can harness self-interest to the public interest. In *Federalist* 51, Madison wrote "Ambition must be made to counter ambition . . . through the whole system of human affairs, private as well as public." But he did not anticipate the great bureaus of American government, and in them his admonition has not been honored. They are not subject to vigorous competition. Much of what state governments spend goes to monopoly bureaus, organizations inherently not disposed toward innovation and efficiency. Requiring public bureaus to compete with private entities for contracts, and granting vouchers or tax credits to citizens rather than funding bureaus directly are the two main ways that more competition could be injected into government. The new economics implies that policymaking for public services *is* designing competition—choice—into their production.

Now, of course humans are not merely the self-interested individuals of economic science. The rigid economic calculus cannot apprehend behavior that arises not from self-interestedness, but instead from altruism. It is confounded by noble politicians, generous entrepreneurs, devoted bureaucrats. But can self-interest be *dependably* transcended: are there circumstances in which people *consistently* act altruistically? Is harnessing self-interest by competition the only reliable policy, the only way of aligning private and public objectives? Or are there policies that will ensure that people will regularly act spontaneously in the interests of others?

Communitarianism is the conviction that humans are not the autonomous, self-interested individuals of economic science, but rather are social creatures, whole only in groups and devoted to others in those groups. The communitarian vision is that people will act, not out of narrow self-interest, but in the interests of the larger group.

Some communitarian hopes must be recognized as commendable but sentimental. Construing a whole state or the entire country as a community, even as a family, is common in political rhetoric, but this understanding lacks persuasiveness and dependability. Indeed, government exists largely because we do not treat others in the polity as we do family members. True, we sometimes are inspired to work toward the public interest. The society needs more of that, but as the American Founders knew, it is folly to construct policy on the assumption that other-mindedness will be consistently forthcoming from businesspeople, politicians, bureaucrats, or ordinary citizens. Such an assumption puts all at the mercy of those who are not so honorably inclined.

Still, in some circumstances people do act to benefit others. Certain groups, particularly those called mediating communities, such as families and religious organizations, have the capacity to draw from many people consistent action in the interests of those with whom they are associated. Perhaps other organizations, neighborhoods and ethnic associations, for example, have that same power. Government bureaus rarely possess this quality. Fortunately, even after all the growth in government and the decline of traditional institutions, most "social services" are performed by mediating communities. Although the bulk of state government spending is devoted to social services, broadly construed, children are raised, the elderly are tended, the infirm are ministered to, mostly outside government, and by people who see themselves doing their duty, rather than performing a service.

There is evidence that some tasks long since thought to have been appropriately turned over to government—schooling is the best example—are often more effectively and less expensively produced in communities than in bureaus. Thus arises the possibility of government's meeting more of its responsibilities—not through bureaus, and not through private firms—through communities. This happens when government transfers spending from educational and medical bureaus (schools and nursing homes) and grants those funds instead to families to expend where they see fit. When the families choose home schooling or religious schools, or when they care for frail loved ones at home, on average society gets equivalent or better results at lower costs. Community supersedes bureaucracy. And a properly operating community provides practice in altruism toward people outside the community; perhaps there is no other way to generate the civic virtue so needed in public life than in healthy private communities.

Neither competition nor community will meet public purposes if not designed properly. Much can go awry in competitive arrangements and in purported communities. But a central theme of this book has been that policymakers need to see their job not merely as budget allocator, or mandator, or exhorter, but also—centrally—as designer of arrangements that accomplish the benefits of competition and community while diminishing their drawbacks.

I believe that many who see the need for government action operate in the unarticulated and unexamined hope that politicians and civil servants will be motivated by consistent public-spiritedness. In that way, they avoid confronting the central question of governance, namely, how does a free society induce private citizens and government employees to act in ways that accomplish public purposes? There will be virtuous politicians and bureaucrats. I have tried to be one. I believe that one justifies one's life through service. Some things do get done by altruists in government. But to state the assumption that virtue pervades public service is to recognize that it is romantic and implausible. Even Jerry Mashaw, America's most potent critic of the new economics of organization, writes that "we seem to lack the capacity for extended sympathy on a continuous basis beyond the family or perhaps the clan. At the very least, the sorry story of much of human history makes it extremely risky to rely on the public spirit as the lodestar of institutional design."[1]

In this book, I have made a case for what seem to me to be the only two dependable means our society has for meeting the great service responsibilities of the states. Any policy for providing those services that does not rely on at least one of those vehicles has to be questioned. Other policies count on either spontaneous good will of government employees or on systematic oversight of government programs by politicians or citizens. The inadequacy of current state services provides ample evidence of the weaknesses of those rationales. Henceforth, those who propose to accomplish government provision of services in ways not depending on either competition or community have the burden of making a plausible case for why their policy should be expected to be efficacious. Of course, there will be government responsibilities that do not lend themselves to either competitive or communitarian means. Parts of the criminal justice system come to mind, as does the articulation and protection of human rights. But that hardly detracts from the necessity to resort to these two powerful means in the areas—the vast bulk of what states do—where they appear to be indispensable.

Both contemporary social science theory and recent experience in America and communist countries tell us that when it comes to providing services, government has only these two powerful, largely self-disciplining instruments for meeting society's objectives. Appropriations of money and strenuous exertions of public-spirited bureaucrats, patriotic managers, and charismatic politicians occasionally have worthwhile effect. But we do not know how to muster those efforts consistently toward public purposes except as they are activated by competition or community, the ways by which government orients our efforts to socially efficacious results. Restructuring government must be understood as designing these two levers into policy. Spending and researching and mandating and managing and exhorting are important, but the critical element is policymaking that designs and uses arrangements that make individual and societal interests congruent.

State policymakers today are challenged to redesign government so as to align the motivations of individuals with public purposes. If they do not do so, the grand responsibilities of state government will not be met. The revenues available to the states are likely to be overwhelmed by demands on their services in the early years of the twenty-first century. We need a constitutional moment, a time when those holding public office reconstruct government. One hopes that the coming fiscal adversity of the states will create that moment, stimulating the public-spiritedness necessary to replace current arrangements with government that works.

# Notes

## Chapter 1

1. Of course, government has other responsibilities besides providing services, but other than income distribution, almost all of state expenditure does go to services. In this book, I am concerned with failures of service provision by markets and by governmental institutions in the sense that these failures permit some persons to benefit unjustifiably at the expense of others or they stand in the way of possible efficiencies or widely beneficial collective action. I call these failures violations of public purpose (see especially chapters 3 and 4). For a discussion of the difficulties of defining the public interest, see David A. Starrett, *Foundations of Public Economics* (Cambridge University Press, 1988), chap. 3, and references there.

2. National Center for Education Statistics, *The Condition of Education 1992* (U.S. Department of Education), p. 130; *Condition of Education 1997*, p. 170; and Bureau of the Census, *Statistical Abstract of the United States 1993* (U.S. Department of Commerce), p. 481.

3. Ibid.

4. John Maynard Keynes, *The General Theory of Employment, Interest and Money* (Macmillan, 1961), p. 383.

5. See Milton Friedman, "The Methodology of Positive Economics," in Friedman, *Essays in Positive Economics* (University of Chicago Press, 1953).

6. Ibid.

7. In recent times some philosophers, notably Herbert Marcuse and Jurgen Habermas, have taken the understanding of social science espoused here to be inherently elitist and antipolitical. These critics contend that a social scientist's choice of subject and method are influenced,

even determined, by the scholar's own prejudices. In their view, basic conceptions and findings of social science emerge from social structure and personal bias. A claim of scientific objectivity is naive, or worse, hypocritical. Out of such criticism, a new kind of policy science, seen by proponents, such as Fay, as a competitor to the dominant mode, is developing. See Brian Fay, *Social Policy and Political Practice* (George Allen and Unwin, 1975). In its most coherent form this new approach emerges from analytic philosophy and critical social theory. Critical social theory is supposed to reveal to members of a society what they are doing when they act or speak in the ways to which they are accustomed. For critical social theory, the truth of a finding is partially determined by whether the people, liberated by their new understanding, act on it. I am unpersuaded. Following Karl Popper, I contend that a theory's assumptions bear no necessary relationship to the desires of those espousing the theory. The method itself of self-consciously thinking of policymaking as the application of theory provides considerable protection against incompetence, deviousness, or imposition of idiosyncratic personal preferences. Explicitness and replicability of procedure tend to bring to light fatuous or ideologically induced assumptions, faulty logic in deriving hypotheses, and dishonest reporting of empirical results. (For politicians this should be a familiar argument. They learn much by listening to competing claims presented in a forum that inhibits dishonesty. In politics, lying is infrequent, not necessarily because people are virtuous, but because they know that the adversarial process in which they are engaged tends to expose fraud.) It is unnecessary and imprudent to choose between policy science as causal hypothesis and policy science as insight followed by liberating action. To me, the Popperian argument that the power of positive science derives from explicitness and replicability, not necessarily from the personal integrity of the scientist, remains persuasive. Furthermore, to offer causal hypotheses does not require the policy scientist to claim to be free of values, nor to believe values to be arbitrary and beyond inquiry. See Herbert Marcuse, *Studies in Critical Philosophy* (London: NLB, 1972); Jurgen Habermas, *Theory and Practice* (Beacon Press, 1973); and Karl Popper, *The Logic of Scientific Discovery* (Basic Books, 1959), chap. 10.

8. There is interesting evidence that economists act more self-interestedly than do other people. See Gerald Marwell and Ruth E. Ames, "Economists Free Ride, Does Anyone Else?" *Journal of Public Economics*, vol.15 (June 1981), pp. 295–310. What is not clear is whether

self-interested people gravitate to that discipline or whether, as Marwell and Ames also conjecture, studying economics leads people to act in the fashion hypothesized by the discipline.

9. Woodrow Wilson, "The Study of Administration," *Political Science Quarterly*, vol. 56 (December 1941), p. 500. The article was originally published in *Political Science Quarterly*, vol. 2 (June 1887), pp. 197–222.

10. Friedman, "Methodology of Positive Economics."

11. David Owen, *Face the Future* (Praeger, 1981), p. 9.

## Chapter 2

1. *Facts and Figures in Government Finance, 1988–1989* (Johns Hopkins University Press, 1988), pp. 46, 169; Advisory Commission on Intergovernmental Relations, *Significant Features of Fiscal Federalism 1994*, vol. 2 (Washington, 1994), pp. 56, 62; and Bureau of the Census, *Statistical Abstract of the United States, 1995* (U.S. Department of Commerce), pp. 299, 459. The description of state and federal spending entails some double counting; over $100 billion of funds spent by state and local governments are grants to them from Washington.

2. For decades, following Richard Musgrave, economists have construed state government as carrying out two broad types of activity: allocative and distributive. The former is meant to consist of activities that improve the efficiency of flawed private markets and the latter supposedly counteracts untoward distributive outcomes of private markets. Thus government is understood as correcting market failure. However, as will be seen in chapter 4, this conception of government as fixer of markets has misled economists and others into perceiving both purpose and efficacy in government, sometimes where there is neither. See Richard Musgrave, *The Theory of Public Finance* (New York: McGraw, 1959). As will become clear in ensuing chapters, the categories used here for presentation of state government activities are hardly arbitrary and were not devised solely for the purpose of shrinking the number of functions to an easily fathomable level. The categories reflect and foretell the theories used in chapter 4 to understand the inefficacy of state government. Measurement without theory is an oxymoron, a point made in a classic article by Tjalling Koopmans. See Tjalling Koopmans, "Measurement without Theory," *Review of Economic Statistics* (August 1947).

3. At that, some of the spending shown as being carried out by the states, for example, state colleges and universities, is largely beyond their management control.

4. Not all that appears in columns A and D is produced by bureaus. Some of the services appearing there are produced by private firms under contract to state or local government. For the definition of a bureau, see William A. Niskanen, *Bureaucracy and Representative Government* (Chicago: Aldine-Atherton, 1971), p. 15; John D. Donahue, *The Privatization Decision* (Basic Books, 1989), pp. 46–48; and Janet Rothenberg Pack, "The Opportunities and Constraints of Privatization," in William T. Gormley Jr., ed., *Privatization and its Alternatives* (University of Wisconsin Press, 1991), pp. 281–306.

5. ACIR, *Significant Features of Fiscal Federalism*, pp. 14, 15.

6. Norman C. Saunders, "The U.S. Economy: Framework for BLS Projections," *Monthly Labor Review*, vol. 116 (November 1993), p. 11; and Thomas Boustead, "The U.S. Economy to 2006," *Monthly Labor Review*, vol. 120 (November 1997), p. 6.

7. Congressional Budget Office, "The Economic and Budget Outlook: Fiscal Years 1997–2006" (May 1996), p. 24; CBO, "The Economic and Budget Outlook: Fiscal Years 1998–2007" (January 1997), p. 14; and CBO, "The Economic and Budget Outlook: An Update" (September 1997), p. 19.

8. *Statistical Abstract, 1995*, p. 399.

9. Bureau of Labor Statistics, "Outlook: 1990–2005" (Department of Labor, 1992); and *Statistical Abstract, 1995*, p. 399.

10. BLS, "Outlook," p. 399.

11. This thesis has been developed in William J. Baumol, Sue Anne Batey, and Edward N. Wolff, *Productivity and American Leadership* (MIT Press, 1989).

12. ACIR, *Significant Features of Fiscal Federalism*, p. 62.

13. Bureau of the Census, "Population Projections of the United States, by Age, Sex, Race, and Hispanic Origin: 1992 to 2050" (Department of Commerce, 1992), pp. vii, viii, 12, 28, 29; and *Statistical Abstract, 1995*, p. 151.

14. *Statistical Abstract, 1995*, pp. 70, 78.

15. Peter L. Benson and Eugene C. Roehlkepartain, "Youth in Single-Parent Families: Risk and Resiliency" (Minneapolis, Search Institute, July 1993), p. 5.

16. See David Blankenhorn, *Fatherless America: Confronting Our Most Urgent Social Problem* (Basic Books, 1995), p. 31, and references there.

17. Elaine Ciulla Kamarck and William A. Galston, "Putting Children First: A Progressive Family Policy for the 1990s" (Washington: Progressive Policy Institute, September 1990), p. 14.

18. Sara McLanahan and Gary Sandefur, *Growing Up with a Single Parent: What Hurts, What Helps* (Harvard University Press, 1994), p. 1.

19. William Duncombe and John Yinger have estimated that to equalize educational outcomes in New York state would require expenditures in large cities to be double the state average. See William Duncombe and John Yinger, "Why Is It So Hard to Help Central City Schools?" *Journal of Policy Analysis and Management,* vol. 16 (Winter 1997), p. 108.

20. David W. Grissmer and others, *Student Achievement and the Changing American Family* (Santa Monica: Rand Corporation, 1994), pp. xxviii, xxxiii, 17, chaps. 5, 6.

21. John Holahan and David Liska, "Reassessing the Outlook for Medicaid Spending Growth," Brief A-6 (Washington: Urban Institute, March 1997), p. 2.

22. Ibid., p. 4.

23. *Statistical Abstract 1995,* p. 210.

24. Stephen Carroll and Eugene Bryton, "Bumpy Ride Ahead for California," *Rand Research Review,* vol. 20 (Summer 1996), p. 12.

25. "Within Our Means: Tough Choices for Government Spending" (St. Paul: Minnesota Planning, 1995), p. 21.

26. ACIR, *Significant Features of Fiscal Federalism,* pp. 30, 31.

27. Ibid., pp. 7, 31. The comparison uses the GDP implicit price deflator.

28. Ibid., pp. 53, 56.

29. See Steven D. Gold, "The Outlook for School Revenue in the Next Five Years," State University of New York, Albany, Center for the Study of the States, Nelson A. Rockefeller Institute of Government, January 1995; and Andrew Reschovsky, "A Balanced Federal Budget: The Effect on States," *LaFollette Policy Report,* University of Wisconsin, Madison (Winter 1997), p. 8.

30. ACIR, *Significant Features of Fiscal Federalism,* pp. 58, 59.

31. Ibid., p. 62.

## Chapter 3

1. Aaron Wildavsky, *The New Politics of the Budgetary Process,* 2d ed. (Glenview, Ill.: Scott, Foresman, 1992), p. xvii.

2. Irene Rubin, *The Politics of Public Budgeting* (Chatham, N. J.: Chatham House, 1990), p. 1.

3. The National Assessment of Educational Progress, *Accelerating Academic Achievement: A Summary of Findings from 20 Years of NAEP* (U.S. Department of Education, 1990), p. 17–18, 20, 21, 22, 26, 62; The National Assessment of Educational Progress, *The Civics Report Card* (U.S. Department of Education, 1990), p. 8, 109; The National Assessment of Educational Progress, *The U.S. History Report Card* (U.S. Department of Education, 1990), p. 109; International Association for the Evaluation of Education Achievement, *The Underachieving Curriculum: Assessing U.S. School Mathematics from an International Perspective* (University of Illinois, 1987), pp. vi, vii; David P. Baker, "Compared to Japan, the U.S. Is a Low Achiever . . . Really: New Evidence and Comment on Westbury," *Educational Researcher*, vol. 22 (April 1993), pp. 18–20; Linda Darling-Hammond, "Achieving Our Goals: Superficial or Structural Reforms?" *Phi Delta Kappan* (December 1990), p. 288; *Digest of Education Statistics* (U.S. Department of Education, 1991), pp. 383–85; Richard J. Murnane and Frank Levy, *Teaching the New Basic Skills: Principles for Educating Children to Thrive in a Changing Economy* (Free Press, 1996), pp. 34–35; and National Center for Education Statistics, *The Condition of Education 1996* (U.S. Department of Education, 1996), p. 88.

4. Allan Odden has compiled the state-by-state changes in real education spending, 1960–90, in "Linkages among School Reform, School Organization and School Finance," University of Southern California, Finance Center of the Consortium for Policy Research in Education, February 18, 1993.

5. In making this comparison I have used the CPI, not an index of education prices. To use the latter would be to conceal the point that it is the increase in expenditure on educational personnel that has driven education spending upward.

6. Bureau of the Census, *Statistical Abstract of the United States 1993* (U.S. Department of Commerce), p. 170.

7. Eric Hanushek, "The Impact of Differential Expenditures on School Performance," *Educational Researcher*, vol. 18 (May 1989), p. 47. The U.S. Department of Education has also found "no correlation between . . . input measures and student achievement." See "Measuring Educational Results," *State Policy Report* (Alexandria, Va.: State Policy Research, July 1989), p. 3.

8. Larry V. Hedges, Richard D. Laine, and Rob Greenwald, "Does Money Matter? A Meta-Analysis of Studies of the Effects of Differential School Inputs on Student Outcomes," *Educational Researcher*, vol. 23 (April 1994), pp. 5–14. See also an exchange between Hedges and others and Hanushek in *Educational Researcher*, vol. 23 (May 1994), pp. 5–8, 9–10.

9. See Stewart C. Purkey and Marshall S. Smith, "Effective Schools: A Review," *Elementary School Journal* (March 1983); W. E. Bickel, "Effective Schools: Knowledge, Dissemination, Inquiry," *Educational Researcher*, vol. 83, no. 4 (1983), pp. 427–52; Herbert J. Walberg, "Educational Strategies That Work," *New Perspectives*, vol. 17 (Winter 1985), pp. 23–26; U.S. Department of Education, *What Works: Research about Teaching and Learning*, 2d ed. (Washington, 1987); and *Accelerating Academic Achievement: A Summary of Findings from Twenty Years of the National Assessment of Educational Progress* (U.S. Department of Education, September 1990).

10. Marshall S. Smith and Jennifer O'Day, reported in "Equality in Education: Progress, Problems and Possibilities," *Policy Brief*, Consortium for Policy Research in Education (New Brunswick, N.J.: Rutgers University, n.d.); and David W. Grissmer and others, *Student Achievement and the Changing American Family* (Santa Monica, Calif.: Rand Corporation, 1994), chaps. 5, 6.

11. Smith and O'Day, "Equality in Education," pp. 5–7.

12. Ibid., p. 8. See also NCES, *Condition of Education 1996*, p. v.

13. Ronald Ferguson, "Racial Patterns in How School and Teacher Quality Affect Achievement and Earnings," Harvard University, John F. Kennedy School of Government, December 1990.

14. David Card and Alan B. Krueger, "School Quality and Black-White Relative Earnings: A Direct Assessment," *Quarterly Journal of Economics*, vol. 107 (February 1992), pp. 51–200. The apparently encouraging finding of Card and Krueger rests on an implausible feature of their statistical model. In their formulation, an increase in spending in any one school district of a state improves the schooling for all students in the state. This would be an acceptable assumption if spending across districts were highly correlated. In fact, the variation in average spending per district is greater within states than is the variation in average spending across states. See Gary Burtless, "Introduction and Summary," in Burtless, ed., *Does Money Matter? The Effect of School Resources on Student Achievement and Adult Success* (Brookings, 1996), pp. 1–2. Evidently the apparently benefi-

cial effects of spending in some states are attributable rather to other characteristics of those states.

15. Ronald F. Ferguson and Helen F. Ladd, "How and Why Money Matters: An Analysis of Alabama Schools," in Ladd, ed., *Holding Schools Accountable: Performance-Based Reform in Education* (Brookings, 1996), pp. 265–98.

16. Dale Ballou and Michael Podgursky, *Teacher Pay and Teacher Quality* (Kalamazoo, Mich.: W.E. Upjohn Institute for Employment Research, 1997), pp. 163, 164.

17. *Digest of Education Statistics*, pp. 72, 88; and Hanushek, "Impact of Differential Expenditures," pp. 45–51, 62.

18. *Digest of Education Statistics*, p. 72.

19. Tommy M. Tomlinson, "Class Size and Public Policy: Politics and Panaceas," *Educational Policy*, vol. 3 (September 1989), p. 263.

20. Debra E. Gerald and William J. Hussar, *Projections of Education Statistics to 2003* (U.S. Department of Education, National Center for Educational Statistics, 1993), p. 3.

21. Daniel Friedlander and Judith M. Gueron, "Are High-Cost Services More Effective than Low-Cost Services: Evidence from Experimental Evaluations of Welfare-to-Work Programs" (New York: Manpower Demonstration Research Corporation, 1990), pp. 3, 5.

22. Barbara J. Stevens, "Comparing Public- and Private-Sector Productive Efficiency: An Analysis of Eight Activities," *National Productivity Review*, vol. 3 (Autumn 1984), p. 398. See also John D. Donahue, *The Privatization Decision* (Basic Books, 1989), especially chap. 4.

23. See David Osborne and Ted Gaebler, *Reinventing Government: How the Entrepreneurial Spirit Is Transforming the Public Sector* (Addison-Wesley, 1992); Harry P. Hatry and Carl F. Valente, "Alternative Service Delivery Approaches Involving Increased Use of the Private Sector," in *The Municipal Yearbook: 1983* (Washington: International City Managment Association, 1983); and John T. Martin, ed., *Contracting Municipal Services: A Guide to Purchase from the Private Sector* (Wiley, 1984).

24. For elaboration of this definition, see Richard J. Zeckhauser and Murray Horn, "The Control and Performance of State-Owned Enterprises," in Paul W. MacAvoy and others, eds., *Privatization and State-Owned Enterprises: Lessons from the United States, Great Britain and Canada* (Boston: Kluwer Academic Publishers, 1989), chap. 1.

25. For elaboration, see Aidan R. Vining and Anthony E. Boardman,

"Ownership and Performance in Competitive Environments: A Comparison of the Performance of Private, Mixed and State-Owned Enterprises," *Journal of Law and Economics* (April 1989).

26. *Statistical Abstract of the United States, 1993*, p. 147.

27. Jeffrey Gilmore, *Price and Quality in Higher Education* (U.S. Department of Education, Office of Educational Research and Improvement, 1990), p. 105.

28. Charles T. Clotfelter, "Explaining the Demand," in Clotfelter and others, eds., *Economic Challenges in Higher Education* (University of Chicago Press, 1991).

29. One impressive effort to determine what part of the earnings differential between college-educated persons and others is due to noncollege factors found that perhaps most of it is due to family background. See J. R. Behrman and others, *Socio-Economic Success* (New York: North Holland, 1980).

30. Clotfelter, "Explaining the Demand," pp. 66, 67. Others have found much higher returns. See the summary in Michael S. McPherson and Morton Owen Schapiro, *Keeping College Affordable: Government and Educational Opportunity* (Brookings, 1991), p. 155.

31. Clotfelter, "Explaining the Demand," p. 67.

32. Malcolm Getz and John J. Siegfried, "Costs per Student over Time," in Clotfelter and others, eds., *Economic Challenges*, p. 390.

33. *Statistical Abstract of the United States, 1993*, p. 150.

34. The remainder of this section draws heavily on Andrew Reschovsky, "Fiscal Equalization and School Finance," *National Tax Journal*, vol. 47 (March 1994), pp. 185–97.

35. See Grissmer and others, *Student Achievement and Changing American Families*.

36. James H. Wyckoff, "The Intrastate Equality of Public Primary and Secondary Education Resources in the U.S., 1980–1987," *Economics of Education Review*, vol. 11 (March 1992), pp. 19, 21. Another study found that in Nebraska "the better is a district's fiscal condition, the higher is the state aid it receives. To be specific, if District A's need-capacity gap is $1 lower than District B's, then District A can expect to receive $0.016 more state aid than District B, all else equal." See Kerri Ratcliffe, Bruce Riddle, and John Yinger, "The Fiscal Condition of School Districts in Nebraska: Is Small Beautiful?" *Economics of Education Review*, vol. 9 , no. 1 (1990), p. 93.

37. The result is reported in Dan Salamone, "An Analysis of State Aid

to Minnesota Cities," Minnesota Taxpayers Association, St. Paul, Minn., August 1992, p. 7.

38. John Yinger, "The Fiscal Condition of Municipal Governments in Nebraska," Occasional Paper 127, Syracuse University, Metropolitan Studies Program, The Maxwell School, March 1988, p. 50.

39. Ronald Fisher, "Income and Grant Effects on Local Expenditure: The Flypaper Effect and Other Difficulties," *Journal of Urban Economics*, vol. 12 (November 1982), p. 324.

40. See Thomas A. Husted, "Changes in State Income Inequality from 1981 to 1987," *Review of Regional Studies*, vol. 21 (Fall 1991), pp. 249–60.

## Chapter 4

1. Charles Murray, *In Pursuit of Happiness and Good Government* (Simon and Schuster, 1988), p. 18.

2. See the historical discussion of the question in Patrick J. Wolf, "The Philosophical Foundations and Historical Development of the American Separation of Powers: Corruption Tamed or Transcended?" Harvard University, Government Department, 1989.

3. See Alexander Hamilton, James Madison, and John Jay, *The Federalist Papers* (New American Library, 1961), especially Numbers 10 and 51, which are generally attributed to Madison.

4. Madison defined a faction as "a number of citizens, whether amounting to a majority or minority of the whole, who are united and actuated by some common impulse of passion, or of interest, adverse to the rights of other citizens, or to the permanent and aggregate interests of the community." Madison in *Federalist* 10, p. 78.

5. See Robert L. Bish, "Federalism: A Market Economics Perspective," *Cato Journal*, vol. 7 (Fall 1987), pp. 377–96.

6. Madison in *Federalist* 51, p. 322.

7. The similarity extends to there being two legislative bodies in each state (except Nebraska, which has only a senate) even though, unlike the national government, representation in both bodies must be on the same basis; that is, all ninety-nine state legislative bodies are apportioned strictly according to population. Typically upper-house districts are twice or three times the size of lower-house districts.

8. See Gaillard Hunt, ed., *The Writings of James Madison*, vol. 5 (New

York: Putnam's Sons, 1904), especially p. 223; and Madison in *Federalist* 53, especially p. 333. In an elegant essay, James Q. Wilson finds in *Federalist* 51 a theory of government based on the self-interested behavior of citizens, and in Federalist 10 a theory that virtue would emerge among leaders of the American republic. See James Q. Wilson, "Interests and Deliberation in the American Republic, or Why James Madison Would Never Have Received the James Madison Award," *PS: Political Science and Politics*, vol. 23 (December 1990), pp. 558–62. In *Making Public Policy: A Hopeful View of American Government* (Basic Books, 1987), Steven Kelman eloquently argues that government in America needs and, in fact, gets much public-spirited behavior from politicians, bureaucrats, and private citizens.

9. Robert Reich sees two "related but conceptually distinct" paradigms dominating public administration in the past forty years: the manager as intermediator among interest groups in a pluralistic society and the manager as maximizer of net benefits using cost-benefit analysis and associated techniques. The two are consistent with the description drawn here of how government has been understood in recent decades. See Robert Reich, "Policy Making in a Democracy: The Limits of Microeconomics," Harvard University, Kennedy School of Government, 1988.

10. I refer here to what economists call *neoclassical welfare economics*, a name with little meaning for those not versed in the discipline.

11. *Facts and Figures in Government Finance, 1988–1989* (Johns Hopkins University Press, 1988), p. 223.

12. The conjecture goes back to Adam Smith and before. In his *The Fable of the Bees*, first published in 1705, Bernard de Mandeville wrote "Vast Numbers throng'd the fruitful Hive; Yet those vast Numbers made 'em thrive; Millions endeavoring to supply Each other's Lust and Vanity; . . . Thus every Part was full of Vice, Yet the whole Mass a Paradise; . . . Then leave Complaints: Fools only strive To make a Great an Honest Hive T' enjoy the World's Conveniences, Be fam'd in War, yet live in Ease, Without great Vices, is a vain EUTOPIA seated in the Brain. Fraud, Luxury and Pride must live, While we the Benefits receive." (Oxford: Clarendon Press, 1924), pp. 18, 24, 36. An exposition in the argot of contemporary economics can be found in Kenneth Arrow, "An Extension of the Classical Theorems of Welfare Economics," in *Proceedings of the Second Berkeley Symposium on Mathematical Statistics* (University of California Press, 1951).

13. It is not certain that government involvement leads to inefficiency.

For a half century and more, some economists have argued that government could determine a desired allocation of resources, then calculate the prices for all goods that, in a market, could yield that allocation, and then, having set those prices, withdraw and permit individuals to respond to the prices, thus bringing about the desired allocation without government's allocating directly. See Oskar Lange and Fred M. Taylor, *On the Economic Theory of Socialism* (University of Minnesota Press, 1938). This possibility will be taken up in chapter 5.

14. A harsh criticism of market failure as rationale for government action has been made, apparently independently, by Richard Nelson, "Roles of Government in a Mixed Economy," *Journal of Policy Analysis and Management*, vol. 6 (Summer 1987), pp. 541–47; and Peter Brown, *Restoring the Public Trust: A Fresh Vision for Progressive Government in America* (Beacon Press, 1994). Both see government not merely as reactive to private sector malfunctioning but as necessary for the functioning of markets and as a "chosen instrumentality" for carrying out some societal responsibilities. See especially Brown, *Restoring the Public Trust*, p. 544.

15. See Charles Wolf Jr., "A Theory of Nonmarket Failure: Framework for Implementation Analysis," *Journal of Law and Economics*, vol. 22 (April 1979), pp. 107–39, for a survey of the inadequacies of competitive markets; and David L. Weimer and Aidan R. Vining, *Policy Analysis: Concepts and Practice* (Prentice Hall, 1989), pp. 39–75, for a more detailed exposition.

16. See A.C. Pigou, *The Economics of Welfare* (London: Macmillan, 1920).

17. For an expanded description of the positive theory of public interest regulation, see Roger G. Noll, "Economic Perspectives on the Politics of Regulation," in Richard Schmalensee and Robert D. Willig, eds., *Handbook of Industrial Organization* (New York: North Holland, 1989), chap. 22. The argument of the positive theory of public interest regulation, that is, "a presumption of efficiency in political practices and public sector arrangements," has been termed the [University of] "Chicago Twist" by Albert Breton, in "Toward a Presumption of Efficiency in Politics," *Public Choice*, vol. 77 (September 1993), pp. 53–65.

18. See P. Dasgupta and Joseph E. Stiglitz, "Potential Competition, Actual Competition and Economic Welfare," *European Economic Review*, vol. 32 (March 1988), pp. 569–77.

19. Personal correspondence with Karl Kurtz, National Conference of State Legislatures, Denver, Colorado; and *Statistical Abstract of the United States, 1993* (U.S. Department of Commerce, 1993), p. 318.

20. *Statistical Abstract, 1993,* p. 160.

21. See Woodrow Wilson, "The Study of Administration," *Political Science Quarterly,* vol. 56 (December 1941), pp. 481–506 (originally published in 1887); and Max Weber, *The Theory of Social and Economic Organization* (Free Press, 1964).

22. Wilson, "Study of Administration," p. 500. Lately a dispute has arisen as to whether Wilson did indeed understand politics and administration to be separate realms. See, for example, Kent Kirwan, "Woodrow Wilson and the Study of Public Administration: Response to Van Riper," and Paul P. Van Riper, "On Woodrow Wilson: Van Riper Replies," *Administration and Society,* vol. 18 (February 1987), pp. 481–506. I believe that Wilson's 1887 essay shows him not necessarily to have held that distinction but to have believed that "constitutional" and "administrative" eras occur in a nation's history and that by the late nineteenth century the United States was past its constitutional period. My argument is that different "constitutions" have different implications for the effectiveness of administration.

23. Max Weber, "Bureaucracy," in Hans Heinrich Gerth and C. Wright Mills, eds., *Max Weber: Essays in Sociology* (Oxford University Press, 1958), p. 214. But see Weber, *Theory of Social and Economic Organization,* for indications of his concern that in the long run bureaus could be counted on to be responsive to political authority.

24. James Coleman, *Foundations of Social Theory* (Harvard University Press, 1990), p. 423.

25. Note that this suggests a greater problem with government's production of services than with its redistribution of income. In the case of income redistribution, persons other than the recipients presumably have less concern with what recipients do with the money because they are not called upon to use it for the benefit of others. In the case of service production, it matters greatly what the teachers, civil servants, and other service producers on whom government money is spent do with it. They are given the money not for their benefit but rather because they are expected to provide some benefit (such as education or day care) to others. But minute by minute, year by year, occasions arise when their interests might conflict with the public's purposes.

26. Jacob Schmookler, *Invention and Economic Growth* (Harvard University Press, 1966), p. 199. Similarly, James Dearden and associates write, "A key obstacle to the adoption of innovations in hierarchical organiza-

tions is not the cost of inventing or developing an innovation but, rather, the cost of constructing incentives to induce agents to adopt the innovation once it is available." See James Dearden, Barry W. Ickes, and Larry Samuelson, "To Innovate or Not to Innovate: Incentives and Innovation in Hierarchies," *American Economic Review*, vol. 80 (December 1990), pp. 1105–24. See also David M. Gould and Roy J. Ruffin, "What Determines Economic Growth?" *Economic Review* (Federal Reserve Bank of Dallas, Second Quarter 1993), pp. 25–40.

27. Terry Moe seems to have invented the term *the new economics of organzation*. See Terry M. Moe, "The New Economics of Organization," *American Journal of Political Science*, vol. 28 (November 1984), pp. 739–77. The theories referred to encompass several subdisciplines, including rational choice theory as it is applied to both public and private sectors (that is, both public choice theory and property rights theory), agency theory, and transaction cost analysis. In all of those theories people are understood as "rent seeking." A rent is a payment for a resource in excess of opportunity cost, that is, over and above the highest valued use to which the resource could be put. Thus rent seeking is the effort devoted to getting from someone else more for a resource than it is worth. The term is usually applied to efforts to get benefits from government, that is, importantly, from persons who make payments from other people's funds, not their own. No comprehensive exposition of the new economics of organization yet exists. Several separate descriptions of the individual subdisciplines have been written, including Dennis Mueller, *Public Choice II* (Cambridge University Press, 1989); Louis De Alessi, "Development of the Property Rights Approach," in Eirik G. Furubotn and Rudolf Richter, eds., *The New Institutional Economics* (Texas A&M University Press, 1991); Douglass C. North, "The New Institutional Economics," *Journal of Institutional and Theoretical Economics*, vol. 142 (March 1986), pp. 230–37; and Oliver E. Williamson, "Transaction- Cost Economics: The Governance of Contractual Relations," *Journal of Law and Economics*, vol. 22 (October 1979), pp. 233–61. Williamson produced a schema on the relationships of the subdisciplines to each other in "A Comparison of Alternative Approaches to Economic Organization," in Furubotn and Richter, eds., *New Institutional Economics*, pp. 104–14. A way of distinguishing among the several subdisciplines, suggested by Williamson, is to consider public choice theory and property rights theory as concerning society's constitution, its fundamental rules and property rights allocations, with the former

theory having to do with public matters and the latter, with private. Then agency theory and transaction cost analysis take up contracting within the broader constitution; agency theory is devoted to considerations at the time of contracting, and transaction cost analysis to how institutions deal with previously unknown developments that typically arise during the course of contract execution.

28. See Bernard Grofman and Donald Wittman, eds., *The Federalist Papers and the New Institutionalism* (New York: Agathon Press, 1989).

29. See Sam Peltzman, "Constituent Interest and Congressional Voting," *Journal of Law and Economics*, vol. 27 (April 1984), pp. 181–210.

30. This is the argument of George Stigler in "The Theory of Economic Regulation," in Kurt R. Leube and Thomas Gale Moore, eds., *The Essence of Stigler* (Stanford, Calif.: Hoover Institute Press, 1986).

31. Terry Moe has elegantly criticized the doctrine of congressional dominance, that is, the argument that the legislative branch controls executive branch bureaus. He contends that other forces, especially a variety of interest groups, exercise influence on both branches. See Terry M. Moe, "An Assessment of the Positive Theory of 'Congressional Dominance,'" *Legislative Studies Quarterly*, vol. 12 (November 1987), pp. 475–520.

32. James D. Gwartney and Richard E. Wagner, "Public Choice and the Conduct of Representative Government," in Gwartney and Wagner, eds., *Public Choice and Constitutional Economics* (Greenwich, Conn.: JAI Press Inc., 1988), p. 18. Gwartney and Wagner add that it is "extremely difficult for a legislative body to control the budget of a bureau and promote operational efficiency" (p. 15).

33. Joseph Kalt and Mark Zupan report evidence of legislators allocating institutional slack not to themselves (as the new economics of organization would predict) but to "rational altruistic-ideological promotion of self-defined notions of the public interest," that is, that they act in some cases out of altruism. Kalt and Zupan, "Capture and Ideology in the Economic Theory of Politics," *American Economic Review*, vol. 74 (June 1984), p. 298. This would not surprise James Madison, but it is an anomaly in the context of the new economics of organization. If legislators act in such a fashion, so might bureaucrats and others. Fostering generous impulses must be part of an agenda for the states; the subject is taken up in chapter 6.

34. James Buchanan, "Public Choice after Socialism," *Public Choice*, vol. 77 (September 1993), p. 69.

35. "Speech to the Electors of Bristol," in B. W. Hill, ed., *Burke on Government, Politics and Society* (New York: International Publications Service, 1976), p. 158. Citizens and even active members of political parties sometimes expect Burkean behavior from their politicians. On the occasion of my leaving the Minnesota Senate I delivered an address to perhaps a thousand delegates and alternates at the Democratic Farmer Labor party convention for the district I represented. I told them that I had tried to see my responsibilities as primarily to the whole of the state and only secondarily to the district I represented. At that point they stopped the speech with applause. It was one of the proudest moments of my life.

36. See Joseph E. Stiglitz, *Whither Socialism* (MIT Press, 1994), chap. 3.

37. *Incontestability* means impossibility of competition. An incontestable advantage enables monopoly. For an expanded discussion of incontestability, see Elizabeth E. Bailey and William J. Baumol, "Deregulation and the Theory of Contestable Markets," *Yale Journal of Regulation*, vol. 1, no. 2 (1984), pp. 111–37. There the important observation is made that if costs to enter and exit a market are low, the market itself may be contestable; a single firm may dominate at any given time, but it may be subject to competition for the whole market.

38. William A. Niskanen, *Bureaucracy and Representative Government* (Chicago: Aldine Atherton, 1971), chap. 4.

39. Andre Blais and Stéphane Dion, "Conclusion: Are Bureaucrats Budget Maximizers?" in Blais and Dion, eds., *The Budget-Maximizing Bureaucrat: Appraisals and Evidence* (University of Pittsburgh Press, 1991), p. 359.

40. The tendency for private markets not to produce public goods can be thought of as still another form of market failure; they are extreme versions of externalities. Two qualities characterize a public good: nonrivalry (if one person consumes it, it remains available for the consumption of others) and nonexcludability (it is not practical to withhold availability, for example, from those who decline to pay for the good). Potential efficiencies and innovations in the production of a public good—and even any production at all—may be frustrated because an individual contemplating producing or improving the good cannot anticipate receiving a return for that effort and cannot prevent "free riders" from reaping the benefits. Thus a lobbying endeavor on behalf of a large number of people, each with a legitimate, but small, complaint might not get organized; a common pasture, fishing bed, or stock of clean air is apt to be overused; potentially beneficial public health measures might not be taken;

and private police services might proliferate where it is in no individual's interest to organize a common effort that would be less costly in the aggregate. Of course, government might undertake to produce public goods not provided by the market, but to do so might, or might not, be in the interests of persons in government and consequently the public goods might, or might not, be provided. Indeed, sometimes quasi-public goods—the airwaves or air traffic control—are provided by government at the instigation of and for the benefit of influential private individuals.

41. See Gary J. Miller and Terry M. Moe, "Bureaucrats, Legislators, and the Size of Government," *American Political Science Review*, vol. 77 (June 1983), pp. 297–322.

42. Recently the Minnesota legislature mandated that all state agencies must implement performance budgeting, measuring their successes against their expenditures. When, after the program was implemented, the Audit Commission staff set out to determine what effect this information was having on legislative decisionmaking, they found that many legislators appeared to have little knowledge at all of the existence of that information. See "Development and Use of the 1994 Agency Performance Reports," State of Minnesota, Program Evaluation Division, Office of the Legislative Auditor, July 1995, pp. 27–28.

43. Kolderie, personal correspondence with the author.

44. This is the so-called property rights hypothesis. See Colin Boyd, "The Comparative Efficiency of State-Owned Enterprises," in Anant R. Negandhi, ed., *Multinational Corporations and State-Owned Enterprises: A New Challenge in International Business*, vol. 1 of *Research in International Business and International Relations* (Greenwich, Conn.: JAI, 1986). Boyd finds evidence inconsistent with the hypothesis. For references to research on the effects of different allocations of property rights, see De Alessi, "Development of the Property Rights Approach."

45. See Stiglitz, *Whither Socialism*, chap. 3.

46. Harvey Leibenstein, "Allocative Efficiency vs. X-Efficiency," *American Economic Review*, vol. 56 (June 1966), pp. 392–415.

47. Charles Wolf, *Markets or Governments* (MIT Press, 1988), p. 66 ff. Wolf invented the term *internalities*. See Wolf, "Theory of Nonmarket Failure."

48. For example, Herbert Simon and others have been determining the implications of assuming that humans have bounded rationality, and an economics of information is merging. See Herbert Simon, "Theories of

Bounded Rationality," in C.B. McGuire and Ray Radner, eds., *Decision and Organization* (Amsterdam: North Holland, 1972). Joseph Stiglitz summarizes what he calls information economics in "Post Walrasian and Post Marxian Economics," *Journal of Economic Perspectives,* vol. 7 (Winter 1993), pp. 108–14.

49. Herbert Simon, cited by Oliver E. Williamson in "The Economics of Governance," in Furubotn and Richter, eds., *New Institutional Economics,* p. 56.

50. Williamson, "Economics of Governance."

51. Stiglitz, *Whither Socialism,* p. 5.

52. One of the subdisciplines of the new economics of organization, principal-agent theory, deals with the asymmetry of information when one individual, the principal, contracts with another, the agent, to carry out some action. Two kinds of problem arise: adverse selection and moral hazard. Adverse selection occurs when a principal, not knowing some relevant information that has been withheld by a prospective agent, contracts with that individual on terms ultimately beneficial to the agent, detrimental to the principal. Moral hazard is the risk that an agent, having been hired, will, if able to get by with it, agree to carry out an action but not do so. See Moe, "New Economics of Organization," pp. 754–56. For an earlier exposition of these problems having to do with asymmetry of information, see Michael Spence and Richard Zeckhauser, "Insurance, Information, and Individual Action," *American Economic Review,* vol. 61 (May 1971), pp. 380–87.

## Chapter 5

1. See the discussion of the Effective Schools Movement in chapter 3.

2. Systemic reform is described in more detail in David K. Cohen, "Standards-Based School Reform: Policy, Practice, and Performance," in Helen F. Ladd, ed., *Holding Schools Accountable: Performance-Based Reform in Education* (Brookings, 1996), pp. 99–127. See also the early article by two of systemic reform's designers and proponents: Jennifer A. O'Day and Marshall S. Smith, "Systemic Reform and Educational Opportunity," in Susan Fuhrman, ed., *Designing Coherent Education Policy: Improving the System* (San Francisco: Jossey-Bass, 1993), pp. 250–312.

3. See Jerry Z. Muller, *Adam Smith in His Time and Ours: Designing the Decent Society* (Macmillan, 1993).

4. Recently several large sectors of the U.S. economy have experienced increased competition after the federal government took deregulatory actions. Empirical estimates of the efficiency savings for the economy find little or no savings in cable television and brokerage, but very large savings in such industries as airlines, railroads, and trucking. See Clifford Winston, "Economic Deregulation: Days of Reckoning for Microeconomists," *Journal of Economic Literature*, vol. 31 (September 1993), pp. 1263–89. Winston describes deregulation as "one of the most important experiments in economic policy of our time" (p. 1263) and concludes that "the evidence clearly shows that microeconomists' predictions that deregulation would produce substantial benefits for Americans have been generally accurate" (p. 1287).

5. See Kenneth J. Arrow, "An Extension of the Basic Theorem of Classical Welfare Economics," in Jerzy Neyman, ed., *Proceedings of the Second Berkeley Symposium on Mathematical Studies and Probability* (University of California Press, 1951); and Kenneth J. Arrow and Gerard Debreu, "Existence of an Equilibrium for a Competitive Economy," *Econometrica*, vol. 22 (July 1954), pp. 265–90.

6. See Peter Murrell, "Can Neoclassical Economics Underpin the Reform of Centrally Planned Economies?" *Journal of Economic Perspectives*, vol. 5 (Fall 1991), pp. 59–76.

7. See John D. Donahue, *The Privatization Decision* (Basic Books, 1989), chap. 5, for an expanded list and discussion.

8. Almarin Phillips, "Comment," *Journal of Policy Analysis and Management*, vol. 6 (Summer 1987), p. 585.

9. John Chamberlin and John Jackson, "Privatization as Institutional Choice," *Journal of Policy Analysis and Management*, vol. 6 (Summer 1987), p. 586.

10. David E. M. Sappington and Joseph E. Stiglitz, "Privatization, Information and Incentives," *Journal of Policy Analysis and Management*, vol. 6 (Summer 1987), p. 568.

11. Ted Kolderie of the Minneapolis-based Center for Policy Studies and Joe Nathan of the University of Minnesota have been the guiding intellect behind the charter schools movement. The most comprehensive description and defense of charter schools is Paul T. Hill, Lawrence C. Pierce, and James W. Guthrie, *Reinventing Public Education: How Contracting Can Transform America's Schools* (University of Chicago Press, 1997).

12. See "An Agenda for Reform: Competition, Community, Concen-

tration: A Report by John Brandl and Vin Weber to Governor Arne H. Carlson," St. Paul, Minnesota Planning, 1995, pp. 17–24.

13. Some economists argue that there is an inherent tendency toward improved efficiency in privatization. See, for example, Maxim Boycko, Andrei Shleifer, and Robert W. Vishny, "A Theory of Privatization," *Economic Journal*, vol. 106 (March 1996), pp. 309–19. They write: "Privatization of public enterprises can raise the cost to politicians of influencing them, since subsidies to private firms necessary to force them to remain inefficient are politically harder to sustain than wasted profits of the state firms. In this way privatization leads to efficient restructuring of firms" (p. 309).

14. See, for example, Oskar Lange and Fred M. Taylor, *On the Economic Theory of Socialism* (University of Minnesota Press, 1938).

15. Joseph Stiglitz argues that central calculation of prices is a practical impossibility. His contention is that perfect competition is not even approximated in real life. Almost every buyer, seller, and product differs in some ways from almost every other. Therefore a near-infinite number of different prices would have to be calculated (by near-omniscient people who would know all those differences). See Stiglitz, *Whither Socialism* (MIT Press, 1994), p. 39.

16. Robert L. Heilbroner, "After Communism," *New Yorker*, September 10, 1990, p. 92.

17. Stipulating property rights also can be useful in enabling conflicts over externalities to be settled by the contending parties, government's role being to determine who has a right to what. For example, if neighbors to a polluting factory have a right to clean air, they might be able to negotiate a settlement with the factory's owner without further government involvement. The factory owner decides whether it is less costly to eliminate the pollution's effects on his neighbors or to satisfy them with payments or in some other way. According to the celebrated Coase theorem, such negotiations can yield efficient outcomes. Coase's argument is of little relevance for policy, however, because it requires not only clearly delineated property rights, but also costless negotiations. See Ronald Coase, "The Problem of Social Cost," *Journal of Law and Economics*, vol. 3 (October 1960), pp. 1–44.

18. Some scholars have contended that the legislative branch wields effective influence over executive branch and other bureaus, but empirical evidence is sparse. See, for example, Barry R. Weingast and Mark J. Moran, "Bureaucratic Discretion or Congressional Control? Regulatory

Policymaking by the Federal Trade Commission," *Journal of Political Economy*, vol. 91 (October 1983), pp. 765–900. Terry M. Moe criticizes the Weingast-Moran argument as resting on a loosely specified model and statistical analysis which yields only ambiguous results. See Terry M. Moe, "An Assessment of the Positive Theory of 'Congressional Dominance,'" *Legislative Studies Quarterly*, vol. 12 (November 1987), pp. 475–520.

19. See James M. Buchanan, Robert D. Tollison, and Gordon Tullock, eds., *Toward a Theory of the Rent Seeking Society* (Texas A&M University Press, 1980).

20. Susan Rose-Ackerman, *Rethinking the Progressive Agenda: The Reform of the American Regulatory State* (Free Press, 1992).

21. James Madison, *Federalist* 51, in Alexander Hamilton, James Madison, and John Jay, *The Federalist Papers* (New York: New American Library, 1961), p. 322.

## Chapter 6

1. A public good is one which, if consumed or enjoyed by one person remains entirely available for others. (See chapter 4, note 40.) For example, under some circumstances any of the following can be a public good: police protection, the services of a lighthouse, language, the products of research, a concert, generosity. In *Collective Action: Theory and Applications* (University of Michigan Press, 1992), p. 196, Todd Sandler summarizes the conditions in which members of a large group might agree to produce a public good. "Successful instances of collective action appear to have one or more of the following features: (a) private or excludable joint products, (b) a pattern of payoffs favorable to dominant players, (c) an exclusion mechanism coupled with a toll scheme, or (d) repeated interactions among players." All of his examples, distilled from the literature of recent decades on the economics of collective action, assume self-interested behavior, so they all entail situations in which individuals are able to reap benefits for themselves greater than the costs they incur (otherwise, under the logic of contemporary economics, they would not undertake the actions). Economists sometimes try to subsume altruism into their calculus by assuming that altruists gain satisfaction from benefiting others. Gary Becker writes "Since an altruist maximizes his own utility . . . he might be called selfish, not altruistic." See Gary Becker, *A Treatise on the*

*Family* (Harvard University Press, 1981), p. 174. Such a construction is circular, unhelpful. In this chapter we are seeking situations where persons, motivated by love or duty, undertake actions benefiting others. In those cases, the costs to themselves might exceed the benefits to themselves. See Samuel P. Oliner and Pearl M. Oliner, *The Altruistic Personality: Rescuers of Jews in Nazi Europe* (Free Press, 1988), for numerous examples. The Oliners are concerned with people who risk life and livelihood to help others, taking actions the explanation for which requires invoking altruism. Daniel M. Hausman and Michael S. McPherson, in a review of the relationship between economics and ethics that is generally sympathetic with neoclassical economics, conclude that "the view of rationality economists endorse—utility theory—may not even be compatible with moral behavior, and it does not provide a rich enough picture of individual choice to permit one to discuss the character, causes, and consequences of moral behavior." See Daniel Hausman and Michael S. McPherson, "Taking Ethics Seriously: Economics and Contemporary Moral Philosophy," *Journal of Economic Literature*, vol. 31 (June 1993), p. 688.

2. Robert H. Frank seems to delight in listing such everyday behavior, which economics is at a loss to explain. See, for example, his "Melding Sociology and Economics: James Coleman's *Foundations of Social Theory*," *Journal of Economic Literature*, vol. 30 (March 1992), p. 153.

3. Douglass North, *Institutions, Institutional Change and Economic Performance* (Cambridge University Press, 1990), p. 140.

4. Kenneth Arrow, "Social Responsibility and Economic Efficiency," *Public Policy*, vol. 21 (Summer 1973), p. 314. Even James Buchanan, an intellectual leader of, and the only Nobel prize recipient among, public choice theorists, emphasizes that "the constraints, rules, and institutions within which persons make choices politically can and do influence the relative importance of the separate motivational elements." Cited in Jane Mansbridge, ed., *Beyond Self-Interest* (University of Chicago Press, 1990), p. 21.

5. Joseph Schumpeter, *Capitalism, Socialism and Democracy* (Harper and Brothers, 1947), p. 207.

6. Mansbridge, *Beyond Self-Interest*, p. ix.

7. Gaillard Hunt, ed., *The Writings of James Madison*, vol. 5 (New York: G.P. Putnam's Sons, 1904), p. 223. Adam Smith also would not endorse the claim that people are nothing but self-concerned. In *The Theory of Moral*

*Sentiments* (Indianapolis: Liberty Classics, 1970), p. 47, he wrote "How selfish soever man may be supposed, there are evidently some principles in his nature, which interest him in the fortune of others, and render their happiness necessary to him, though he derives nothing from it, except the pleasure of seeing it."

8. The usual definition of a community is an organization whose members perceive their ends as common. See Allen E. Buchanan, "Assessing the Communitarian Critique of Liberalism," *Ethics*, vol. 99 (July 1989), pp. 852–82, and references there. I prefer the definition in the text above because I wish to emphasize the possibility of government's using communities to bring benefits to some persons by encouraging the community membership of others.

9. See Alasdair MacIntyre, *After Virtue: A Study in Moral Theory* (University of Notre Dame Press, 1981), pp. 204–05. MacIntyre has written, "In spite of rumors to the contrary, I am not and never have been a communitarian." "I'm Not a Communitarian, But . . . ," *The Responsive Community: Rights and Responsibilities,* vol. 1 (Summer 1991), p. 91. Despite his declaration, I term him a communitarian, and for two reasons. His is a communitarian critique of liberalism. And he wishes for a more communitarian society (but believes that to be most unlikely). He fears that communitarian efforts could backfire into totalitarianism. His reason for rejecting being called a communitarian is that current conditions in America and the West are so wretchedly libertarian as to "exclude the possibility of realizing any of the worthwhile types of political community which at various times in the past have been achieved" (p. 91).

10. MacIntyre, *After Virtue*, p. 156, and *Whose Justice? Which Rationality?* (University of Notre Dame Press, 1988), especially chap. 4 in which, referring to Athens in the fifth century, B.C., he extols a vision of the individual's not being complete unless deeply involved in public affairs. Also see Steven Kelman, *Making Public Policy: A Hopeful View of American Government* (Basic Books, 1987). As Kelman's subtitle suggests, he finds many politicians resisting the temptation merely to be agents of parochial interests.

11. See MacIntyre, *After Virtue*; and Michael J. Sandel, *Liberalism and the Limits of Justice* (Cambridge University Press, 1982), p. 11. Sandel here expresses the stated criticism in a form that he later rejects, but his rejection is for the purpose of giving his attack on liberalism deeper grounding.

12. John Rawls, *A Theory of Justice* (Harvard University Press, 1971), p. 192.

13. Allen E. Buchanan, "Assessing the Communitarian Critique of Liberalism," *Ethics*, vol. 99 (July 1989), p. 858.

14. Sandel, *Liberalism and the Limits of Justice*, p. 64.

15. Thomas Nagel, "Rawls on Justice," in Norman Daniels, *Reading Rawls: Critical Studies on Rawls' A Theory of Justice* (Basic Books, 1975), pp. 9–10.

16. The following owes much to Robert Booth Fowler's classifications and discussion of communitarian thought, though some of my categories are different from his, and readers will detect differences in our understandings of republican community. See Robert Booth Fowler's *The Dance with Community: The Contemporary Debate in American Political Thought* (University Press of Kansas, 1991).

17. See Amitai Etzioni, *The Moral Dimension: Toward A New Economics* (Free Press, 1988); and *The Spirit of Community: Rights, Responsibilities and the Communitarian Agenda* (Crown, 1993).

18. Etzioni, *The Spirit of Community*, p. 5.

19. Cited by William A. Schambra in his foreword to Robert Nisbet, *The Quest for Community: A Study in the Ethics of Order and Freedom* (San Francisco: Institute for Contemporary Studies, 1990), pp. xiv, xi.

20. See Friedrich Hayek, *The Road to Serfdom* (London: Routledge and Kegan Paul, 1962; first published 1944), especially chap. 2.

21. Robert Heilbroner, "After Communism," *New Yorker*, September 10, 1990, p. 96.

22. Cited in Schambra, foreword, in Nisbet, *Quest for Community*, p. x.

23. Fowler, *Dance with Community*, p. 64.

24. See Gordon S. Wood, *The Creation of the American Republic 1776–1787* (Norton, 1972); Robert N. Bellah, and others, *Habits of the Heart: Individualism and Commitments in American Life* (University of California Press, 1985); and J. G. A. Pocock, *The Machiavellian Moment: Florentine Political Thought and the Atlantic Republican Tradition* (Princeton University Press, 1975).

25. Locke himself was no celebrator of unbridled self-interest. He "condemn[ed] the unregulated pursuit of self-interest that Hobbes considered natural." James T. Kloppenberg, "The Virtues of Liberalism: Christianity, Republicanism, and Ethics in Early American Political Discourse," *Journal of American History*, vol. 74 (June 1987), p. 16. Locke wrote, "He that

has not a mastery over his inclinations . . . he that knows not how to resist the importunity of present pleasure, or pain, for the sake of what reason tells him, is fit to be donne, wants the true principle of Vertue, and industry; and is in danger never to be good for anything" (p. 16). Kloppenberg sees religion, classical republicanism, and liberalism all influencing the Founders of the American Republic. All require individuals to be subject to constraints on self-interest. Indeed, Kloppenberg writes that "laissez-faire liberalism was not present at the creation of the American republic but emerged over the course of the nation's first hundred years" (p. 29).

26. See especially Robert Putnam, "Bowling Alone: America's Declining Social Capital," *Current*, vol. 6 (June 1995), pp. 65–78.

27. Peter Berkowitz, "The Art of Association," *New Republic*, June 24, 1996, p. 47.

28. Madison in Alexander Hamilton, James Madison, and John Jay, *The Federalist Papers* (New American Library, 1961), Number 51, p. 322.

29. Plato, *The Republic*, trans. by H. Spens (New York: E. P. Dutton, 1911); also see George H. Sabine, *A History of Political Theory* (New York: Henry Holt, 1950), chaps. 3, 4.

30. George F. Will, *Statecraft as Soulcraft* (Simon and Schuster, 1983), p. 27.

31. This sentence does not apply to Douglass North, who studies the formation of cultural norms and institutions. See North, *Institutions, Institutional Change and Economic Performance*.

32. John Patrick Diggins, *The Lost Soul of American Politics: Virtue, Self-Interest, and the Foundations of Liberalism* (University of Chicago Press, 1984), p. 296.

33. See J. Milton Yinger, *Countercultures: The Promise and the Peril of a World Turned Upside Down* (Free Press, 1982). Yinger evidently invented the term *counterculture* in 1960 or before. He prefers contraculture, but uses both forms of the term, having, he says, "like Mark Twain, . . . no sympathy for those ignorant people who know only one way to spell a word" (pp. xi, 3).

34. See especially Roberto M. Unger, *Politics: A Work in Constructive Social Theory* (Cambridge University Press, 1987).

35. See Kirkpatrick Sale, *Human Scale* (New York: Coward, McCann and Geoghegan, 1980).

36. See Rosabeth Moss Kanter, *Commitment and Community: Communes and Utopias in Sociological Perspective* (Harvard University Press, 1972).

37. Fowler, *Dance with Community*, pp. 45–52.

38. See Schambra, foreword, in Nisbet, *Quest for Community*, p. xiii; and Jane J. Mansbridge, *Beyond Adversary Democracy* (Basic Books, 1980), pp. 299, 341.

39. Sale, *Human Scale*.

40. Some offshoots of feminism, however, that perceive community as suspect cannot be understood as types of participatory community: Susan Okin, for example, fears community as a trap. She sees freedom, especially for women, as fundamental and fundamentally at odds with losing oneself in any group. To her, communities, including the family, are means of accomplishing female subjugation. See Susan Okin, *Justice, Gender, and the Family* (Basic Books, 1989).

41. Boyte is prolific. See Sara M. Evans and Harry C. Boyte, *Free Spaces: The Sources of Democratic Change in America* (Harper and Row, 1986); Harry C. Boyte, *Commonwealth* (Free Press, 1989); and "Remapping Democratic Politics," University of Minnesota, Hubert H. Humphrey Institute of Public Affairs.

42. Boyte, "Remapping," p. 25; and Boyte, *Commonwealth*, pp. 20, 89, 190.

43. Boyte, "Redefining Politics, Part II," *The Responsive Community: Rights and Responsibilities*, vol. 3 (Spring 1993), p. 86.

44. Boyte, "Remapping," p. 26.

45. Mansbridge, *Beyond Adversary Democracy*, p. vii.

46. Ibid., pp. 292, 293, 300.

47. Ibid., pp. xii, xiii.

48. Peter L. Berger and Richard John Neuhaus, *To Empower People: The Role of Mediating Structures in Public Policy* (Washington: American Enterprise Institute for Public Policy Research, 1977), pp. 2, 6.

49. Becker, *Treatise on the Family*, p. 195.

50. Jeffrey M. Berry, Kent E. Portney, and Ken Thomson, *The Rebirth of Urban Democracy* (Brookings, 1993), p. 284.

51. James S. Coleman and Thomas Hoffer, *Public and Private High Schools: The Impact of Communities* (Basic Books, 1987), p. 213. As will be seen below, Coleman and Hoffer conjecture that the differential efficacy of public and Catholic schools is due not to Catholicism in particular but to the communities found in some religious schools.

52. Ibid., pp. 33, 212, 213, 219.

53. William N. Evans and Robert M. Schwab, "Finishing High School and Starting College: Do Catholic Schools Make a Difference?" University of Maryland, Department of Economics, November 1993, p. i.

54. Derek Neal, "The Effect of Catholic Secondary Schooling on Educational Attainment," Working Paper 5353 (Cambridge, Mass.: National Bureau of Economic Research, November 1995), pp. i, 25, 31.

55. See Jay P. Greene, "Civic Values in Public and Private Schools," in Paul E. Peterson and Bryan C. Hassel, eds., *Learning from School Choice* (Brookings, forthcoming). Greene arrives at these conclusions using data from the National Education Longitudinal Study. He does find that though private schools are better integrated by race, they are considerably less well integrated by income except for Catholic schools, which mirror the income levels of the areas in which they are located.

56. Ronald F. Ferguson and Helen F. Ladd find that "community-based interventions can make a tremendous difference." Ferguson and Ladd, "How and Why Money Matters: An Analysis of Alabama Schols," in Ladd, ed., *Holding Schools Accountable: Performance-Based Reform in Education* (Brookings, 1996), p. 276.

57. Sara McLanahan and Gary Sandefur, *Growing Up with a Single Parent: What Hurts, What Helps* (Harvard University Press, 1994), p. 121 ff.

58. Anthony S. Bryk, Valerie E. Lee, and Peter B. Holland, *Catholic Schools and the Common Good* (Harvard University Press, 1993), p. 16 ff.

59. Ibid., p. 39.

60. Nathan Glazer, "American Public Education, The Relevance of Choice," *Phi Delta Kappan*, vol. 74 (April 1993), pp. 647–50.

61. Paul T. Hill, Gail E. Foster, and Tamar Gendler, "High Schools with Character," Rand Report R-3944-RC (Santa Monica, Calif.; Rand Corporation, 1990), p. ix.

62. Coleman and Hoffer, *Public and Private High Schools*, pp. 214, 239, chap. 8.

63. See Dan Coats, "When Redistribution and Economic Growth Fail," *The Responsive Community*, vol. 6 (Winter 1995–96), p. 6.

64. T. David Evans and others, "Religion and Crime Reexamined: The Impact of Religion, Secular Controls, and Social Ecology on Adult Criminality," *Criminology*, vol. 33 (May 1995), pp. 195–224.

65. Marc A. Musick, "Religion and Subjective Health among Black and White Elders," *The Journal of Health and Social Behavior*, vol. 37 (September 1996), p. 221; and Amy L. Sherman, "Cross Purposes: Will Conserva-

tive Welfare Reform Corrupt Religious Charities?" *Policy Review*, no. 74 (Fall 1995), p. 58.

66. Robert Putnam, "Bowling Alone, Revisited," *The Responsive Community*, vol. 5 (Spring 1995), pp. 18–33.

67. Burton A. Weisbrod and Mark Schlesinger, "Public, Private, Nonprofit Ownership and the Response to Asymmetric Information: The Case of Nursing Homes," in Susan Rose-Ackerman, ed., *The Economics of Nonprofit Institutions: Studies in Structure and Policy* (Oxford University Press, 1986), pp. 133–51.

68. Peter Uhlenberg, "Replacing the Nursing Home," *The Public Interest*, no. 128 (Summer 1997), p. 78.

69. Michael J. Donahue and Peter L. Benson, "Religion and the Well-Being of Adolescents," *Journal of Social Issues*, vol. 51 (Summer 1995), p. 145.

70. James S. Coleman, *Foundations of Social Theory* (Harvard University Press, 1990), p. 251.

71. William C. Mitchell, "The Shape of Public Choice to Come: Some Predictions and Advice," *Public Choice*, vol. 77 (September 1993), p. 141.

72. Robert Putnam refers to religion as "by far the most common associational membership among Americans." See Putnam, "Bowling Alone, Revisited," p. 22.

73. Amartya Sen, "The Formulation of Rational Choice," *American Economic Review*, vol. 84 (May 1994), p. 389.

74. Mary Ann Glendon, "Law, Laws, and Human Community," *First Things*, no. 4 (June–July 1990), p. 28.

75. See Peter F. Drucker, "Reflections of a Social Ecologist," *Society*, vol. 29 (May–June 1992), pp. 57–64, who writes of nonprofit organizations that "these institutions discharge [an] . . . important task in American society: they provide effective citizenship. In modern society, direct citizenship is no longer possible. All we can do is vote and pay taxes. As volunteers in the nonprofit institutions we are again citizens; we can have an impact on social order, social values, social behavior, social vision. . . . The nonprofit institution thus increasingly creates citizenship and community" (p. 60).

76. See Burton A. Weisbrod, *The Nonprofit Economy* (Harvard University Press, 1988); and Avner Ben-Ner and Benedetto Gui, eds., *The Nonprofit Sector in the Mixed Economy* (University of Michigan Press, 1993), for economic analyses of the behavior of nonprofit organizations.

## Chapter 7

1. Janet Weiss makes a version of this point, saying that "leadership is not only a conceptual morass; it also has sharply limited implications for policy. Good leaders are scarce, and cannot even be counted upon to replicate their own successes," "Ideas and Inducements in Mental Health Policy," *Journal of Policy Analysis and Management*, vol. 9 (Spring 1990), pp. 196–97.

2. See Howard Davies, *Fighting Leviathan: Building Social Markets That Work* (London: Social Market Foundation, 1992).

3. The term *purchaser-provider split* seems to have been coined in Great Britain. See ibid. Ted Kolderie has suggested that the term *provider* be reserved for the entity that takes responsibility for seeing to it that a service exists; thus for social markets the provider is the government agency funding and organizing the market. Following Kolderie, I here use the term *purchaser-producer split* to denote the importance of separating buyer and seller. See Ted Kolderie, "The Two Different Concepts of Privatization," *Public Administration Review*, vol. 6 (July–August, 1986), pp. 285–91.

4. Burton A. Weisbrod, "Rewarding Performance That Is Hard to Measure: The Private Nonprofit Sector," *Science*, May 5, 1989, p. 244.

5. John McKnight, *The Careless Society: Community and Its Counterfeits* (Basic Books, 1995).

6. Cited in Stuart M. Butler, "Practical Principles," in Michael Novak, ed., *To Empower People* (Washington, AEI Press, 1996), p. 116. Berger and Neuhaus write that "we underestimated the degree of corruption that comes with government funding, not, of course, corruption in the sense of criminal misuse of funds (that is a relatively manageable matter) but the much more insidious corruption in which these institutions reshape themselves to continue as beneficiaries of government largesse." "Peter Berger and Richard John Neuhaus Respond" (ibid., p. 150).

7. "Peter Berger and Richard John Neuhaus Respond," p. 50.

8. Michael Sandel, "America's Search for a New Public Philosophy," *Atlantic Monthly*, March 1996, p. 70; Mary Ann Glendon, review of Michael J. Sandel, *Democracy's Discontent: America in Search of a Public Philosophy* in *New Republic*, April 1, 1966, p. 41; and Michael Sandel, "The Politics of Community: Robert F. Kennedy versus Ronald Reagan," *The Responsive Community*, vol. 6 (Spring 1996), p. 16.

9. To this point I have described a policy of government funding for community production of services. There are, however, several other ways in which government influences communities. Eugene Steuerle, noting that the income tax exemption for a child is now about one-fourth its real value of a half century ago, and that the marriage penalty under the tax laws results in a 25 percent differential in income for a cohabiting unmarried couple over an otherwise similarly placed married couple, argues that government policy penalizes families by making both marriage and childbearing more expensive. Eugene Steuerle, "Tax Credits and Family Values," *The Responsive Community*, vol. 5 (Summer 1995), pp. 44–49. William A. Schambra argues for "a massive assault on the credentialing and regulatory barriers that suppress citizen-building, grassroots initiatives, barriers more often than not erected by professional service-providers [with government funds] chiefly to protect their prerogatives." William Schambra, "To Be Citizens Again," *First Things*, no. 65 (August–September 1996), p. 17. Mary Ann Mason sees the no-fault divorce laws now in effect in all states as not only facilitating breakup of families but contributing to a situation where "divorced men experience an average 42 percent rise in their standard of living while the standard of living for divorced women and their dependent children declines by an average of 73 percent." Mary Ann Mason, "The De-Regulation of Family Law: In Whose Best Interests?" *The Responsive Community*, vol. 3 (Spring 1993), p. 45.

10. See Michael Novak, *The Spirit of Democratic Capitalism* (Simon and Schuster, 1982), pp. 129, 143 ff. Like Berger and Neuhaus, Novak includes a wider variety of organizations in his definition of mediating structure. I use a narrower definition of mediating communities (organizations in which people are dependably drawn to seek the welfare of others) because I wish to make use of that altruism in carrying out societal responsibilities through those communities assisted by government.

11. Thomas J. Kane, "Comments on Chapters Five and Six," in Helen F. Ladd, ed., *Holding Schools Accountable: Performance- Based Reform in Education* (Brookings, 1996), p. 209.

## Chapter 8

1. Jerry L. Mashaw, *Greed, Chaos, and Governance: Using Public Choice to Improve Public Law* (Yale University Press, 1997), p. 27.

# Index

Altruistic behavior: and
self-interest, 92–93, 162–63n. 1;
social capital and, 111–12
Arrow, Kenneth, 81–82, 93
Asymmetry of information, 72,
159n. 52

Ballou, Dale, 34
Becker, Gary, 106
Bellah, Robert, 99
Benson, Peter L., 111
Berger, Peter L., 105–06, 125
Berkowitz, Peter, 100
Bounded rationality, 72
Boyte, Harry, 103–04
Bryk, Anthony S., 109
Buchanan, Allen E., 95
Buchanan, James, 62
Budget deficit, federal, 25–27
Budgets: as government policy,
29–30; for higher education, 39;
limitations of, 134; maximizing
attempts, 67
Bureaucracy: budget-maximizing
attempts by, 67; failures of (*see*
Organizational failure); lobbying
activities, 61; monopolistic, 74;
neutral competence view of, 53–
54; for policy implementation,
52–53; self-interested behavior
of, 48–49
Bureaucratic inefficiency, 35-38
Burke, Edmund, 63

Chamberlin, John, 83
Charter schools, 84
Choice: in social markets, 116–18,
122. *See also* Competition
Churchill, Winston, 98
Clotfelter, Charles, 40
Coase theorem, 161n. 17
Coleman, James, 53, 107, 108, 110,
111
Communitarianism: defined, 94,
138; versus liberalism, 94–95
Community: complementarity with
competition, 127–28; described,
12–13; and feminism, 167n. 40;
as government instrument, 2,
139; inclusive, 96–99; mediating,
97, 105–14, 138; participatory,
101–05; as policy, 9; republican,
99–101; voluntary associations
and, 100
Community service production:
incentives for, 127, 171n. 9;
independent monitoring, 127; indirect finance element, 123, 125,

129; nondistribution constraint to, 113, 126, 129; underfunding of services, 126–27, 129
Competition: charter schools experiment, 84; complementarity with community, 127–28; direct, 82; diversions, 81–82; as government instrument, 2, 139; and innovation, 82, 84; Madison's view of, 47, 80–81, 137; and market efficiency, 50–51; mediated, 82–83; monitoring, 82; versus monopoly, 65, 157n. 37; as policy, 9; and privatization, 84–85; as self-interest restraint, 81. *See also* Social markets
Corrections expenditures, 25
Cost-benefit analysis, by judiciary, 89-90
Critical social theory, 142–43n. 7
Croly, Herbert, 99
Cuomo, Mario, 97

Debreu, Gerard, 81–82
Debureaucratization in social markets, 119–20
Diggins, John Patrick, 101
Direct competition, 82
Distracted monitoring, 68–71
Diversions, and competition, 81–82
Donahue, Michael J., 111

Economics of organization: competition, 9, 80–85; described, 11–12; importance of, 87–88, 136; in policymaking, 76–80; price adjusting, 85–87, 136–37; principal-agent theory, 159n. 52; property rights, 161n. 17; reformulation of, 55–56; Weber's view of bureaucracy, 53

Education: achievement failures, 30–31; charter schools experiment, 84; demographic influences on, 22–24; expenditures for, 2–3; expenditures versus results, 31–35, 39–40, 77; experimental schools project, 54; higher education funding, 39; local funding, 41–43; power equalization, 42; religious schools, role of, 107–10; and systemic reform, 80
Effective Schools Movement, 32, 34
Etzioni, Amitai, 96–97
Evans, William N., 108
Experimental schools project, 54

Ferguson, Ronald, 33, 34
Fisher, Ronald, 44
"Flypaper effect," 44
Ford Foundation, 37
Fowler, Robert Booth, 99, 102
Friedlander, Daniel, 36
Friedman, Milton, 10

Gilmore, Jeffrey, 39
Glazer, Nathan, 109
Glendon, Mary Ann, 113
Gueron, Judith M., 36

Hanushek, Eric, 31
Harvard University, 37
Hayek, Friedrich, 98
Health care expenditures, 24–25, 26
Heilbroner, Robert, 99
Higher education funding, 39
Hill, Paul, 109
Hoffer, Thomas, 107, 108, 110, 111
Holland, Peter B., 109

Incentives: for community service production, 127n. 9; importance

of, 77–79; in social markets, 120–21, 129
Inclusive community, 96–99
Independent monitoring: of community services, 127; of social markets, 121, 129
Indirect government finance, 123, 125, 129
Information asymmetries, 72, 159n. 52

Jackson, John, 83
John F. Kennedy School of Government, 37
Johnson, Lyndon B., 97
Judiciary, cost-benefit analysis by, 89–90

Kane, Thomas J., 128
Kennedy, John F., 98
Keynes, John Maynard, 5
King, Martin Luther, 98
Kolderie, Ted, 69

Labor productivity, 21
Ladd, Helen, 33, 34, 43
Lee, Valerie E., 109
Legislative oversight, 68–71
Legislators: and bureaucratic lobbying, 61; parochial interests of, 6, 57–61, 88–89; self-interested behavior of, 46–47; unproductive behavior of, 62–63
Leibenstein, Harvey, 71
Liberalism: criticisms of, 95; defined, 94; versus communitarianism, 94–95
Lobbying by public employees, 61

MacIntyre, Alasdair, 95
McKnight, John, 123

McLanahan, Sara, 23
Madison, James, 12; competition, view of, 47, 61, 80–81, 137; and government failure, 135; leadership qualities, need for, 48, 56; on balance of powers, 47; on public virtue, 93–94; and republican community, 100
Management, as policy substitute, 78
Manpower Demonstration Research Corporation (MDRC), 35
Mansbridge, Jane, 93, 104
Maritain, Jacques, 109
Market failure: effects of, 135; as government action rationale, 49, 50–52; monopoly and, 65–66; in public finance theory, 49; and public goods production, 157–58n. 40; sources of, 63–65; from unpriced goods and services, 66–68. *See also* Organizational failure
Mashaw, Jerry, 140
MDRC (Manpower Demonstration Research Corporation), 35
Mediated competition, 82, 83
Mediating communities, 97, 105–14, 138; religious schools as, 107–10
Mediating structures: defined, 105; flawed or criminal, 125
Mitchell, William C., 112
Mondale, Walter, 97
Monitoring: and competition, 82; distracted, 68–71
Monopoly, 64, 65–66, 74
Murray, Charles, 46

NAEP (National Assessment of Educational Progress), 30
Nagel, Thomas, 95

National Assessment of Educational Progress (NAEP), 30
Neal, Derek, 108
Negative externality, 67–68
Neuhaus, Richard John, 105–06, 125
Neutral competence view of bureaucrats, 53–54
Niskanen, William A., 67
Nondistribution constraint, 113, 126, 129
North, Douglass, 93
Novak, Michael, 127

Organizational failure: distracted monitoring, 68–71; effects of, 135; and internal orientation, 71–72; monopoly and, 65–66; sources of, 63–65; from unpriced goods and services, 66–68. *See also* Market failure
Organization theory. *See* Economics of organization
Owen, David, 14

Participatory community, 101–05
Phillips, Almarin, 83
Pigou, A.C., 51
Plato, 101
Pocock, J.G.A., 99
Podgursky, Michael, 34
Policymaking: budget role in, 29–30; competition, role of, 80–85; as design of government, 76–80; price setting, 85–87, 136–37; and self-interest theory, 6–8; for societal objectives, 1–2, 76–77; and systemic reform, 80; theory versus pragmatism, 4–5
Populism, as participatory community, 103

Positive theory of public interest regulation, 51–52
Price setting, 85–87, 136–37
Principal-agent theory, 159n. 52
Principled oversight, 89–90
Privatization, 84–85
Public finance theory: government action in, 51; and market failure, 49
Public good, defined, 162n. 1
Purchaser-producer split, 118–19, 129, 170n.3

Rand Corporation, 23
Rational choice theory, 111
Rawls, John, 95
Religious schools, effectiveness of, 107–10
Rent seeking, 89, 155n.27
Republican community, 99–101
Rivlin, Alice, 54
Rose-Ackerman, Susan, 89
Rubin, Irene, 29

Sale, Kirkpatrick, 103
Sandefur, Gary, 23
Sandel, Michael, 95, 125
Sappington, David, 83
Schmookler, Jacob, 55
Schumpeter, Joseph, 93
Schwab, Robert M., 108
Self-interest: and altruistic behavior, 92–93, 162–63n.1; limitations of, 12; and new economics of organization, 55–56; and policymaking, 6–8; and separation of powers, 47–49; social harm from, 51
Sen, Amartya, 112
Separation of powers, and self-interested behavior, 47–49
Smith, Adam, 47, 80–81, 137

Social capital, 111–12

Social markets: choice, element of, 116-18, 122; competition-inducing policies for, 122–23; debureaucratization and, 119–20; defined, 116; incentives for, 120–21, 129; independent monitoring of, 121, 129; purchaser-producer split, 118–19, 129, 170n. 3. *See also* Competition

State government: allocative and distributive functions, 144n. 2; budget as policy, 29–30; bureaucratic inefficiency, 35; choice and community agenda, 129–32; economic growth prospects, 19–22, 134; entitlement programs growth, 22; expenditure allocations, 17–19, 57–58, 60; expenditures and outcomes, 5–6; federal aid to, 25–27; growth of, 16; local government funding, 41, 43–44; policymaking objectives, 76–80; policymaking responsibilities of, 1–2; and production of services, 154n. 25

State-owned enterprises, 38–39

Stevens, Barbara, 36

Stiglitz, Joseph, 72, 83

Systemic reform, 80

Underfunding of services, 126–27, 129

Unpriced goods and services, 66–68

Voluntary associations, 100

Weber, Max, 50, 53

Weisbrod, Burton, 123

Wildavsky, Aaron, 29

Will, George, 101

Williamson, Oliver, 72

Wilson, Woodrow, 9, 50, 53

Wolf, Charles, 71

Wood, Gordon, 99

Woodson, Robert, 123, 125

Yinger, John, 43